COLLINS

CAMCORDER HANDBOOK

SHOOT the VIDEO

CAMCORDER HANDBOOK

A beginner's guide to making better home videos

STEVE PARKER

SHOOT the VIDEO

LIMITED EDITIONS
BOOKTITLES

ACKNOWLEDGEMENTS

The author would like to thank the Walt Disney Company, Commodore UK, Brian Smith and John Hill Associates for their assistance in the production of this book.

The four-part television series, *Shoot the Video*, was written and produced by David John Hare and is a JR Production in association with Fuji Tape.

Videos of *Shoot the Video* are available from Teaching Art Ltd, PO Box 50, Newark, Notts NG23 5GY

This edition published in 1995
by Limited Editions

First published in 1993 by
HarperCollins Publishers, London
Reprinted 1994

Photographs: Shona Wood

Illustrations: Rt Illustrators

Edited, designed and typeset by Haldane•Mason, London

A catalogue record for this book is available from the British Library

Printed and bound in Slovenia

ISBN 0 583 31893 2

Foreword

by Chris Serle

Welcome to the exciting world of video, where, with the aid of a camcorder, you can produce a permanent record of all the important events in the life of your family, from holidays and weddings to keeping a record of your children as they grow. Or you can embark on more ambitious projects, producing and directing your own home movies. Whatever you use your camcorder for, this marvellously sophisticated piece of equipment opens the door to the fastest-growing hobby of the moment.

When you work in television, as I do, you get to see all the techniques and secrets that make the difference between an interesting and professional-looking TV programme and one that looks, quite frankly, amateurish. In the TV series *Shoot the Video*, I reveal some of the shooting and editing secrets used by the professionals. In this *Handbook*, we explore them in greater detail, explaining how you can make the most of your camcorder and the useful accessories that are available to help you in your movie-making.

The book also contains several pages that tie in with each episode of *Shoot the Video*, showing you some of the simple techniques for recording holidays, weddings, children and documentaries.

Remember, above all, that camcorders are great fun – so long as you don't let them overshadow the event you are recording. Aim to enjoy the moment, while recording it so that you can enjoy it again and again afterwards.

Contents

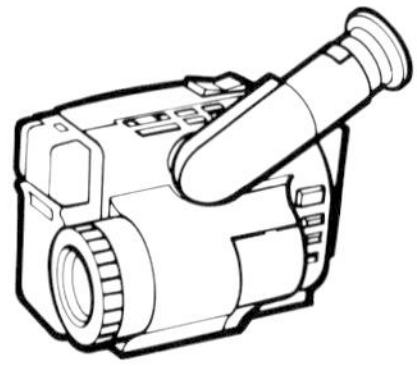

3 EDITING · 72

4 EDITING AND ENHANCING EQUIPMENT · 100

5 SOUND · 132

Introduction

When you watch television or a movie at the cinema, you rarely notice the camera technique. This is because the director does everything to make it as unobtrusive as possible. This enables you to enjoy the story, without being constantly reminded you are looking at a film set, surrounded by camera, lighting and sound operators, actors, key grips, dolly grips and best boys.

When you pick up your camcorder, you take the place of the director. You probably find your first attempts at making a home movie look a bit shaky – but don't worry. This isn't because you don't have the movie director's large budgets and expensive equipment. It is because movie-makers have learned the tricks of the trade that enable them to produce slick and professional movies.

You can learn these tricks too. The same basic techniques apply whether you are shooting a kids' party or are on the set of *Spartacus*, surrounded by a cast and crew of thousands.

The *Collins Camcorder Handbook* is an easy-to-understand guide to the basic techniques of home video. It is

designed for people who are completely new to camcorders, but in later chapters deals with more advanced techniques to help you improve your skills further.

How the book works

The book is divided into five sections.

- Part one shows you how to ensure a steady image, choose the best composition for your subject and move smoothly while recording.
- Part two looks at camcorder controls and tells you when to let the camcorder make decisions for you, and when to step in to take creative control. It also discusses using filters and additional lights to enhance the image.
- Part three shows you how to make your home movies interesting, structuring your shots to tell a story.
- Part four takes a comprehensive look at the mechanics of editing, including adding titles to give your videos professional polish.
- Part five looks at sound recording techniques and assesses the different kinds of add-on microphone. It is followed by information on caring for your equipment and a glossary of terms used in the book.

The *Collins Camcorder Handbook* will become an indispensable part of your equipment. The information is presented in a clear and easy to follow way, to provide the ideal reference guide to using your camcorder.

The *Collins Camcorder Handbook* accompanies *Shoot the Video*, the video and television series presented by Chris Serle. Easily identifiable sections in the book look at each episode and explain the techniques used by Chris to produce interesting, watchable movies on the four subjects covered: holidays, weddings, children and documentary videos.

Bar

1

Getting Started

Handling
Supports
The Zoom Lens
Composition
People
Shot Size
Camera Angles
Framing
Panning
Tilting
Perspective
Dollying
Tracking
Arcing

HANDLING

If your home videos look shaky compared with the pictures you watch on TV, you're not alone. The single most important factor that separates amateur videos from professional productions is the steadiness of the image.

Image stabilization

Keeping the image steady isn't easy. Practise holding the camcorder as still as possible while recording. Stand with your feet slightly apart, toes pointing outwards. Grip the camcorder tightly with both hands, and pull your elbows into your chest.

You will find that, while camera shake is less noticeable on wide-angle shots, every tiny movement of the camcorder is exaggerated on the telephoto setting.

Whenever possible, minimize camera shake by moving closer to the subject rather than zooming in.

Left: Unless using a shoulder-mounted camcorder, grip the camcorder tightly with both hands. Your right hand slips inside the supporting strap, with your first two fingers resting on the electronic zoom control. Your thumb operates the record button.

Right: The main job of your left hand is to make sure the camcorder is held steady. On some camcorders, the more advanced controls are positioned on the left-hand side, so you can operate them while giving the camcorder support.

Whenever you are out and about with your camcorder, make use of any natural support you can find. The camcorder is only as steady as you are, so if you lean against a wall or tree (*above*) the shots are steadier.

Ideally, rest the camcorder – or your elbows – on top of a solid surface, such as a wall or car roof (*above right*). Sitting or lying down gives you extra support, too. Lean your elbows on your knees when sitting (*right*) and on the ground when lying (*below*) to give you the firmest support.

SUPPORTS

Virtually all camcorders have a tripod mount. This is a small round socket on its base into which you can thread accessories to give the camcorder extra stability.

The simplest such support is the pistol grip. This screws into the bottom of the camcorder, giving it the appearance of a large handgun – but it should never be held like one. The right hand holds the camcorder normally, while the left clasps the grip.

Camcorders can also be attached to chest pods. These have a central pole to give support, with a harness which goes around the user's neck for extra stability. If you are thinking about buying one, try a few first to see which feels most comfortable.

Monopods

More popular are monopods. These consist of a single pole that screws into the tripod mount and rests on the ground. They are very light, which makes them particularly suited to situations where you need to move from one location to another.

It is important that you hold the monopod perfectly upright, otherwise the shot may look crooked. For added stability, rest the pole against your foot or body. Hold the camcorder with your right hand in the usual way, and take a firm grip of the monopod with your left hand.

The advantage of a monopod is that it is lightweight and easily portable. Make sure you don't hold the monopod at an angle, otherwise the shot will be crooked.

Tripods

The steadiest support is the tripod, which has three legs and a central pole that can be adjusted up or down. Some models have rubber bases on each leg that screw back to reveal sharp spikes for use on grass and other soft outdoor surfaces.

If you buy a support, take into consideration its portability as well as its stabilizing effect.

TRIPODS

Tripods are the sure-fire method of ensuring your pictures are steady. Buy one that is rigid and can easily take the weight of your camcorder.

Some tripods need a separate tripod head. This is the platform that sits between the camcorder and the tripod. A good tripod head can be locked, so that it doesn't move if you knock it by accident. It should also be able to move smoothly when you want to swivel the camcorder while it is recording.

STEADICAM JR

The Steadicam JR is the junior version of a device used by professional movie crews. Its job is to keep the camcorder steady while the operator is moving and recording.

Using a system of weights and counter-weights, the Steadicam JR makes sure the camcorder is kept level, even when the operator is running. A black and white monitor is built into the device so you don't have to hold the camcorder's viewfinder to your eye.

Steadicam JR is best used for following moving subjects using the wide-angle end of the lens.

THE ZOOM LENS

All camcorders have zoom lenses built in. When you press the telephoto control on your camcorder, your subject is magnified. This is called zooming in.

Even the most basic camcorders have 6x zoom lenses. With a 6x zoom, an object in the viewfinder appears 6x wider and 6x higher at the telephoto setting than at the wide-angle. Many camcorders have more powerful zooms, such as 8x, 10x and 15x.

With such a versatile tool, it is tempting to use it while recording, but it's easy to overuse or misuse the facility. After shaky images, overuse of the zoom lens is the second biggest fault of home videos.

Cropping tool

The main function of the zoom lens is as a cropping tool. Zoom in until you get the most attractive composition, and crop out all the unwanted scene around it. Only start recording when you have the shot you want.

Lens converters

With long telephotos, you can also fill the frame with subjects that are far away. If you find that the wide-angle lens on your camcorder isn't wide enough for your needs or the telephoto lens isn't long enough, you can buy a lens converter. Lens converters attach to the end of the camcorder's lens and modify it so that the telephotos appear even longer and the wide-angles even wider.

Each wide-angle converter or tele-converter has a number attached to it called a conversion factor. For example, a teleconverter with a 2x conversion factor doubles the magnification of the subject, turning a 6x zoom into a 12x zoom.

Although camcorders have very long telephoto lenses, the wide-angle is sometimes neglected. Most camcorders would not be able to record this scene without a wide-angle converter.

This is the view you would get from the wide-angle settings on most camcorders. It is adequate for outdoor work, but could be limiting if you wanted to shoot in confined indoor locations.

If you want to feature a particular subject in the scene you are videoing, zoom in to get the exact crop you want. This crop shows a point midway along the zoom range.

You can select any magnification between the wide-angle and the telephoto settings, so you can exactly frame the portion of the scene you want.

The telephoto of even the least impressive zoom range is generally powerful enough to pull in fairly distant subjects.

For extremely distant subjects to fill the frame you need a camcorder with an extended zoom range or a teleconverter attached to the end of your lens.

Teleconverters magnify the image by a number known as a conversion factor. A conversion factor of 2x doubles the size of the image. Converters up to 12x are available.

FOCAL LENGTHS

If you look at the specification of your camcorder in your instruction manual, you will see the zoom range expressed as a set of figures. These are known as focal lengths and are measured in millimetres.

A 6x zoom might be designated a 9–54 mm zoom. This means the focal length is 9 mm at the wide-angle setting and 54 mm at the telephoto end. If you are familiar with still cameras, you will know the standard lens on an SLR is 50 mm. At this setting the subject appears about the same size in the frame as it does to your eye.

Your instruction manual will also tell you the size of the imaging chip in your camcorder – either 1/3 in, 1/2 in or 2/3 in. For camcorders with 1/3 in imaging chips, around 5.7 mm is equivalent to the photographic 50 mm lens. With 1/2 in and 2/3 in imaging chips, the equivalents are 8.6 mm and 11 mm respectively. This means the average camcorder with a 6x zoom lens has a focal length range equivalent to a 50–300 mm zoom on a still camera.

COMPOSITION

When you have no control over the subjects you are recording, composition is simply choosing which lens setting to use and where to stand to record the best image. If you do have control over the subjects, composition also involves deciding how they should be arranged.

There are few rights and wrongs. You have to judge the attractiveness of each option yourself. There are guidelines to help you decide: don't include unnecessary parts of the scene; crop in close unless showing the whole scene is important; watch out for distracting subjects.

Before you start recording, scan the scene for problems, both through the viewfinder and directly. Red is a particularly distracting colour.

1

2

3

1 Here, the focal length is too wide, and unnecessary background is included. The subject would look better if cropped closer.

2 The choice of shooting position is suspect because the building looks very flat when viewed from this angle.

3 This is a more attractive crop: the subject is properly framed with no distracting elements.

RULE OF THIRDS

Both painters and photographers have learned that subjects tend to look more attractive if they are placed a third of the way in from the edge of the frame, rather than at the centre. This has become known as the Rule of Thirds.

If you look at paintings or professional photographs, you will see this tendency arise again and again.

Placing the horizon
When recording a shot that includes the horizon, for instance, it is common practice to place it either a third of the way down the frame or a third of the way up from the bottom.

For example, if the important subject-matter is on the ground, then the horizon should be placed a third of the way from the top. If the important action is in the air, however – such as rolling clouds or aeroplanes – the horizon should be placed a third of the way up from the bottom of the frame.

DEPTH

Our eyes see slightly different views of a scene, which helps us to perceive depth. TV screens are flat, so subjects at different depths may appear to be the same distance away.

This can give rise to problems such as poles appearing to grow out of people's heads. Scan the frame to avoid these.

You can add the illusion of depth to your shots by using lead-in lines. These are straight lines, such as the sides of a path, that converge into the frame.

PEOPLE

Many shots in video contain people. The rules of composition apply equally to people as they do to inanimate objects.

Even when a person looks straight into the camcorder lens, the shot may look better if they are standing a third of the way in from the edge of the frame, rather than in the centre.

Cut-off points

Unless your shot contains the whole person, you have to cut them off at the bottom of the frame. The point on the body where the person is cut off by the frame is known as the cut-off point.

There are better cut-off points than others. Most parts of the body are fine, but avoid truncating the subject at the neck, waist, knees or ankles, as these compositions look unattractive.

The most commonly used cut-off points are around the armpits, slightly above and below the waist and just above the knees.

Viewer–subject intimacy

Although there is no reason why you can't record people from behind, the general custom is to shoot them from the front or side. This builds up a much greater feeling of intimacy between the viewer and the subject.

The idea of viewer–subject intimacy is very important in video, as your aim is to produce a video that holds the viewer's attention. If you shoot a subject from the back or side, the viewer tends to feel like an outsider.

If you record the subject looking straight into the lens, however, you can build up a rapport between the viewer and the subject.

When including part of a person in the frame, avoid cutting them off at the neck, waist, knees or ankles. The cut-off points that give the best compositions are shown here.

LOOKING ROOM

When shooting a person like this boy, the viewer tends to follow his eyes in the direction they are looking, so it is usual to compose people so they are facing the centre of the frame. The space in front of them is known as looking room.

If you shoot the boy so he has his back to the centre of the frame, the viewer follows his eyes straight out of the TV screen. The part of the frame behind his head is known as redundant space. There should be more looking room in the frame than redundant space.

A lot of space behind someone's head suggests there is something interesting happening behind him, off screen.

HEADROOM

The Rule of Thirds applies particularly to head-and-shoulders shots of people. When you record such a shot, the subject, such as this juggler, looks far more natural if his eyes are a third of the way down from the top of the frame.

If you compose the shot so that the juggler's eyes are below half-way down the frame, he appears to be sinking off the bottom of the TV screen. This is known as having too much headroom. If his eyes are higher in the frame, he may look too cramped.

By keeping the eyes at the same point in the frame, you ensure the person's head doesn't bob up and down.

SHOT SIZE

As everything you shoot on video is viewed on a two-dimensional TV screen, no subject can be physically closer to the viewer than any other. However, you can increase a subject's apparent closeness (and thereby its impact) by making it larger in the frame by either moving the camcorder closer to the subject or zooming in.

The amount of the frame occupied by the subject is described in terms of shot size. All subjects can be described by their shot size, but the term is usually used about people.

Video makers divide shots into five main sizes: extreme long shot (ELS), long shot (LS), mid shot (MS), close-up (CU) and extreme close-up (ECU).

EXTREME LONG SHOT

The extreme long shot (ELS) is also known as the vista shot. That's because it's usually used to show a wide location to establish where the action is set. Any people in an ELS are usually very small.

One of the ways of making your home movies easier to follow is to include an ELS of the location every time the action moves to a different place. The ELS can also be used to show impressive landscapes and cityscapes or the view from a tall building or aeroplane.

LONG SHOT

A long shot (LS) of a person includes the whole body. Normally, it is better to move in closer than this, but the shot is useful if you want to show a group of people or a specific location, such as a building.

An LS of people should contain enough of the location to show where the action takes place. Shooting in LS makes it easy for the viewer to follow what is happening, but if you never move closer than LS, they may find it difficult to get involved in the action.

MID SHOT

The mid shot (MS) cuts off people just below the waist. A variation, the medium close-up (MCU), cuts off just above the waist. In many respects, this is the most versatile shot size. When you frame someone in MS, you are far enough away to capture their arm gestures, but close enough to see their facial expressions.

Another variation on the MS, the two shot, includes two people cut off just below the waist. This shot shows conversations without having to switch from one person to the other.

CLOSE-UP

Close-ups (CUs) enable us to get close enough to a person to see their facial expressions in detail. The cut-off point is normally around the armpits. Don't be afraid to zoom in close, but don't get so close that movements of the person's head take them out of the frame.

CUs can have a lot of impact. If the person is expressing emotion, such as laughter or sorrow, the viewer is far more likely to react than if it is recorded in LS. The CU is also used to show inanimate objects, especially writing, in detail.

EXTREME CLOSE-UP

Extreme close-ups (ECUs) have even more impact than CUs. They are used to concentrate attention on a small detail in a scene.

In human terms, an ECU might contain from just below the mouth to just above the eyes. Only use such a shot if the action is very dramatic or the person is saying something important.

As eyes are extremely expressive, an ECU of eyes filling the screen can be a very powerful way of expressing an emotion or thought without using words.

CAMERA ANGLES

Most adults can be shot from your own head height as this is the correct height for them too. If they are seated, however, you will have to crouch down to keep the camcorder level with their head.

When shooting children you should hold the camera at their head height, not your own. Otherwise, you have difficulty engaging the viewer's sympathy. This may entail crouching or even lying on the floor.

Most people hold the camcorder at their own head height when recording. As the majority of adults are of similar height, it means the camcorder doesn't need to be angled up or down. The most natural way of viewing a subject is with the camcorder held level. This kind of shot is called a neutral shot.

Shooting at different levels

When you are shooting a subject taller or shorter than yourself, you should still try to hold the camcorder level. This means that, for a seated person, you should sit down yourself or crouch so you are shooting from their level.

Children, too, should be shot from their own height, not from above. Kneel or sit down to record them.

If you are recording two subjects with different head heights, shoot from the height of the one you want the audience to associate with. Some children's programmes, for instance, are shot from children's head height, so that all adults on the screen appear tall and dominating.

Just as moving in from LS to CU increases the viewer's association with the subject, moving the camcorder closer to the person's head height also builds viewer-association with the subject.

If you shoot from a different camera angle, you weaken the link between the viewer and the subject, just as you do when you shoot in ELS. Looking down on a landscape puts the viewer in the role of impartial observer.

If you are shooting small pets or toddlers playing on the floor, crouch down so you shoot them from their height. However, you may make babies look appealing and vulnerable if you shoot them from above.

LOOKING UP

You can alter your subject's appearance by shooting from above or below. Looking up at a subject can make it appear more important or stronger in the frame.

If you want to shoot a neutral shot of a tall building, stand some way away and use the telephoto. If you want to draw attention to its height, stand close and point the camcorder up.

People look stronger when you shoot them from below, because they are looking down on the viewer. This is known as subject strength–viewer weakness. People also appear taller than their surroundings when shot from below, which reinforces their power on the screen.

If you lower the camera angle only slightly, you may simply make the person appear taller.

LOOKING DOWN

By shooting from above, you can make a subject appear weaker or less significant than it is. When you record people from above, the camcorder looks down, putting the viewer in a position of strength: viewer strength–subject weakness.

Video people from above to make them look lonely or scared. Animals shot from above can look cute, rather than weak.

Shooting from a very high angle, such as a tall building, removes the viewer from the action. Called scrutiny shots, the viewer takes in the scene without feeling involved in what is going on.

Angry exchanges are often shot from below, heightening the tension through subject strength–viewer weakness, while intimate scenes often use a less threatening high camera angle.

FRAMING

Keeping the camcorder level while recording is important. If the horizon is slightly crooked, the viewer notices and it draws attention away from the subject.

There are occasions, however, when having a deliberately crooked horizon can be used creatively. Recording with the camcorder held diagonally to the ground – canting the frame – is sometimes referred to as the Dutch Tilt.

Holding the camcorder parallel to the ground is the norm because that's how we are used to seeing the world. If lines we consider as horizontal or vertical are shown as diagonals in the frame, the images look more dynamic.

If you cant the camera only slightly, the shot may look like a mistake. You need to cant the camera by 30° or more to achieve the right effect.

Using the Dutch Tilt

The Dutch Tilt is often used with moving subjects to emphasize speed. Try standing at a bend in the road looking back at cars speeding towards you. Record the cars with the camcorder held level, then cant the frame by about 40° and make a second recording. Notice how the shots look more dramatic with the Dutch Tilt. Canting can be used with static subjects to emphasize untidiness.

FRAMES WITHIN FRAMES

The main limitation on video composition is the television-screen format, which is four units wide by three deep. This 4:3 relationship is known as the TV's aspect ratio.

If you have a subject that is taller than it is wide, you can't turn the camcorder through 90° to get a more appealing composition because you can't rotate the TV. You can, however, create a frame within a frame, drawing the viewer's attention to the subject inside the frame.

Doors, mirrors and archways are the most common frames. The effect of looking through one of these is to give viewers the impression they are spying, or to show a scene from the subject's point of view.

DIAGONAL COMPOSITION

To overcome the problem of TV screens being two-dimensional, frame a subject to emphasize its depth. If you shoot a building from the front, for instance, there are no clues to indicate that you are looking at a three-dimensional scene.

If you change position slightly, so that you are standing at the corner of the building, you see both the front and one side. As you are shooting neither straight on, the horizontal lines of the floor and roof appear to converge, adding the depth you need.

If you can frame a scene so that you can see objects which are clearly at different depths in the frame, you will add a complete illusion of depth. The illusion of depth is known as presence.

PANNING

Keeping the camcorder still while recording is essential if you are to make professional-looking home videos. But in some instances, it is better to move the camcorder while recording. Standing in the same position while moving the camcorder horizontally is known as panning.

Moving subjects and landscapes
One of the principal reasons for panning is to keep a moving subject correctly composed. If you shoot a moving person, you have to pan the camcorder simply to keep them in the same position in the frame.

Panning can be used to show a location that is too wide to fit into a single static shot. Even if you could fit in a whole panorama by using a wide-angle lens, the pan has the advantage that you can use a telephoto lens and get closer to the objects in the scene.

Another use for the pan is to reveal the various parts of a scene one by one, so the viewer doesn't have to search the whole screen picking out the points of interest.

The pan can also be used to move from one subject in a scene to another. This explains to the viewer how the two subjects relate to each other.

Lead-in pans
The lead-in pan combines the other types of pan shot, and is often used by professional movie-makers to start a scene. The camcorder begins by panning with a moving subject, then comes to rest on a second subject. The first subject then moves out of shot.

Here, the second subject is the important one. The first is used merely as a device to show the location and set the scene before moving to more important matters.

Panning technique
Make sure the panning movement is smooth and that you don't overshoot. Unless following a moving subject, end the pan on something interesting.

If you can, use a tripod with a fluid movement pan and tilt head. Hold a static shot for a few seconds at the start and end of a pan.

You can show a wide location in far more detail with a pan shot than you can with a static wide-angle shot. Hold the static shots at the start and end of the pan for a short while before you begin the movement.

For a pan such as this, you get the best results by using a tripod with a pan and tilt head. When you pan using a tripod, keep your feet firmly planted throughout the shot. Just as you leave looking room in front of a static person, when panning you should leave moving room in front of a moving subject for it to move into.

HOW TO PAN

When not using a tripod, you can achieve the smoothest pan by twisting your body from the hips, rather than the shoulders.

- Work out where you are going to start and end your pan, then stand with your legs slightly apart, facing in the direction you intend to end your pan.
- Twist your body until you are pointing in the direction in which you want to start the pan. Press the record button.
- Hold the shot for a couple of seconds, then slowly unwind your body until you are again facing the front. Record for a few more seconds then pause. You will find it tricky to pan more than 90°.

TILTING

Tilting is a specialized form of panning, where the camcorder moves up and down, rather than from left to right or right to left. It is sometimes called the vertical pan.

Shooting tall buildings

The tilt is most commonly used for subjects that are too tall to fit in a single static shot, such as high buildings. As with pans, you should end the tilt on an interesting subject. If you are tilting down a building, this might be the doorway. If you are tilting up, you might end on a person leaning out of a window.

Practise tilting and playing back the results. A gentle tilt down a tall building should take 5–6 seconds.

If you want to make the building look even taller than it is, use the telephoto end of the lens. As the frame contains a lot less of the subject than with a wide-angle, slight movements are exaggerated.

You can also draw attention to a building's height by standing close to it. The closer you are, the greater the angle you have to tilt the camcorder to include the top.

People and tilts

Tilts can be used dramatically or humorously to emphasize a person's height or power. If you start with their feet, then slowly tilt up until you reach their face, you can make them seem incredibly tall.

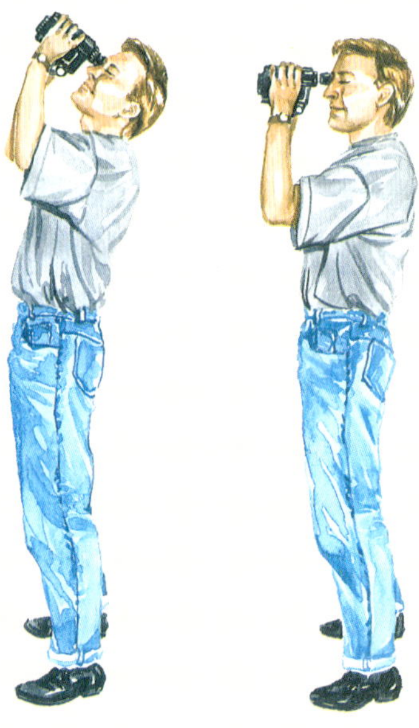

HOW TO TILT

Tilts must be carried out smoothly or the viewer will notice the poor technique. If you are handholding the camcorder, tilt your body from the waist, not the shoulders.

- Tilt up until you can see the top of the subject.
- Start recording and hold the shot for a few seconds.
- Slowly tilt your body down until the camcorder is level.
- Hold the shot, then pause.

Make sure horizontal lines in the scene are parallel with the bottom of the frame throughout the shot.

MOVING SUBJECTS

Tilts are used for following moving subjects less often than pans because fewer things move vertically than move horizontally.

You can probably tilt smoothly to follow a space rocket or a person diving off a high diving-board, but most subjects that move up or down do so more erratically.

Fortunately, with a slow-moving subject, the speed and smoothness of the tilt are not as important as when you are tilting down a building.

Treat tilting to follow a moving subject as you would panning to keep a subject correctly composed. If you are videoing somebody climbing a staircase, for instance, simply tilt the camcorder to keep them at the same position in the frame.

Hosepiping
Normally, it is not advisable to follow a pan or tilt with a pan or tilt in the opposite direction. This is called hosepiping and tends to make the viewer feel seasick.

When you pan or tilt with a moving subject, however, the viewer's eyes remain fixed on the subject, so you can pan and tilt freely. For instance, when you watch a recorded football match, you follow the ball with your eyes and are hardly aware that the camcorder is constantly panning and tilting to follow the action.

PERSPECTIVE

As you zoom from wide-angle to telephoto, subjects in the frame's centre appear to get larger. With the telephoto lens, everything seems closer than it is. If you keep your lens on the wide-angle setting and move physically closer to your subject, it again occupies more of the frame.

In both instances the subject gets larger, but the results look entirely different, as you can see in the pictures. When you frame a subject, you have to decide whether to use a wide-angle lens and stand close, use a telephoto and stand farther away, or choose a combination in between.

1 Wide-angle lens/ distant subject.
2 Standard lens/ distant subject.
3 Telephoto lens/ distant subject.
4 Wide-angle lens/ semi-distant subject.
5 Wide-angle lens/ close subject.
1 **2** **3** Zooming in: the subject is magnified with no change in perspective.
1 **4** **5** Moving in: perspective changes.

Using a wide-angle and standing close isolates the subject from its surroundings. Using a telephoto and standing further away makes subjects at different distances appear closer together. The difference in a subject's appearance when seen from different positions is known as perspective.

2

3

Zooming in

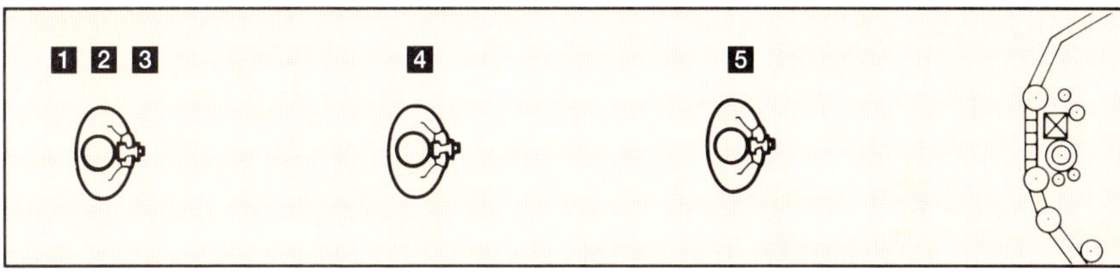

Moving in

4

5

Zooming and perspective

Perspective has important implications for zooming the lens while recording. When you zoom, the perspective doesn't change, as every item in the scene remains in the same position relative to the others.

When you move closer, however, the perspective does change. Closer subjects move towards you and past you, out of the frame, more quickly.

Zooming gives no real impression of movement, and is often a poor option to physically moving the camcorder. But just as you can pan and tilt slightly to keep a subject correctly composed, so you can zoom in and out discretely.

Indiscriminate zooming in and out is called tromboning and should be avoided if you want to produce a professional-looking video.

DOLLYING

Static shots and pans are relatively easy to master, as you can remain in the same position throughout. With a little practice, keeping moving shots steady becomes easy too.

When you first start using your camcorder, it is tempting to go beyond panning and record while walking. If you do, every movement of your body is passed on to the camcorder. Keeping the shot steady in these conditions can be difficult.

Well-executed moving-camera shots can look impressive. They are known as dolly shots, after the wheeled platforms the professionals use to move their cameras while recording.

One of the advantages of dolly shots is that they enable you to explore a scene in detail. Pans can scan a scene in seconds, but mostly the subject is too far away to be seen in any detail.

Apart from its advantage over zooms, which don't show changes in perspective, with a dolly shot you can move round corners and through doors. This makes them far more versatile than other shots.

Shaky camera work detracts from the action, so generally dolly shots should be smooth. But if you are trying to show somebody's point of view as they walk, a slight jerkiness helps create the effect.

TRIPOD DOLLIES

The best way of ensuring steady moving-camcorder shots is with a Steadicam JR (see p. 15). A cheaper, less versatile, alternative is the tripod dolly.

This consists of three wheels attached to a metal frame. The legs of a tripod clip on to the dolly and are firmly secured. The right hand controls the camcorder, while the left steers the tripod.

Tripod dollies need a smooth surface to travel over, so they can only be used on rough terrain if you lay down boards for them to run along.

As exact framing is imprecise, stick with the wide-angle when dollying.

REVEALING A SCENE

Different shot sizes create different effects. With an LS, viewers are removed from the action. With a CU they are drawn into it.

If you dolly or zoom the camcorder towards or away from a subject, you change its shot size during the movement. Dollying towards or away from a subject is known as trucking.

Increasing tension
By moving from an LS to a CU, you can create a build-up of tension. In drama productions, the build-up generated by trucking in is often used to heighten tense or intimate scenes. Dollying in quickly is often used to show a moment of realization on the part of the character.

Increasing authority
Trucking slowly towards a person can heighten their apparent authority. You can exaggerate this by lowering the camcorder height. In LS, the low shooting angle isn't noticed, but as you get closer, you have to tilt the camcorder up to keep the correct composition.

Focusing attention
When you truck in, you focus attention on the subject. When you truck or zoom out, it is the location that is important.

Moving out from CU to LS reveals more of the location throughout the shot. It is particularly effective if the subject is in an unexpected location.

TRACKING

Dollying the camcorder to follow a moving subject is known as tracking. With a pan you can only follow a subject if it is moving in a relatively straight line and if there is no obstruction between you and it.

With a tracking shot, you can follow a moving subject wherever it goes. More importantly, you can remain the same distance from it throughout the shot. This allows you to maintain the subject's shot size and composition in the frame.

When you are videoing a conversation between two people walking along, the only way you can keep them in MS is to use a tracking shot. If you pan with them or stand a long way in front of them and use a static shot, they are in LS for much of the time, which lessens the impact of what they are saying on the viewer.

Professional video-makers use either a Steadicam or a set of mini-railway tracks to produce a smooth dolly. You can use a tripod dolly or improvise with any object that has castors and can take the weight of either you or you and a tripod.

Wheelchairs, shopping trollies and office chairs all make passable dollies. With all these, you need someone to push you along. In the movies, this person is called the dolly grip.

EXPLORING A SCENE

You can use a tracking shot to move in a straight line to show a broad location. For example, moving along street shop-fronts or tracking to show a landscape.

Advantages of tracking

Tracking in this way is similar to panning to show a location. The big advantage of the track over the pan is that it enables you to see each part of the scene in detail. This is not possible with the pan because when the camcorder is fixed there are always parts of the scene that are farther away than others.

The advantage of tracking over showing each of the subjects as separate static shots is that you can show how the various subjects relate to each other.

INDIAN-GROUCHO WALK

If you want to truck towards a subject without a dolly, you have to keep the camcorder as level as possible. The Indian-Groucho walk lets you move forward without your head bobbing up and down. Bend your legs, crouch slightly and lean forward. Make sure your heels touch the ground before your toes, as this removes the spring from your step.

Natural dollies
Setting up a dolly to move smoothly along a street or landscape is difficult, so make use of natural dollies. Trains can be excellent vehicles for shots of urban or rural landscapes. As long as the road is smooth, cars, too, can be used as dollies. But don't lean out of the window or do anything that could lead to an accident.

Crane shots
Vertical dollies (crane shots) can be very effective: the viewer feels elevated by a crane up and deflated by a crane down.

Cranes are difficult without equipment. Improvise by using a glass elevator or fork lift truck. Alternatively, wind up the central column of a tripod or lift yourself from a crouch to tiptoe while recording.

ARCING

Another use for the moving camera is to examine a stationary subject or group of subjects from more than one angle. Moving the camcorder in a circular motion around a subject is called arcing.

Arcing serves another purpose as well as inspection. In dramatic terms it increases the importance of the subject inside the arc, drawing a distinction between it and the subjects outside the circle, and heightens its significance in the video.

Arcing is also a more interesting way of viewing a subject. If you are faced with a statue or monument, for instance, a still camera can only shoot it from one side. With your camcorder you can move round the subject, examining it from all angles, as well as seeing the entire location where it is situated.

Graphically, the shot looks better if the subject is kept in the centre of the frame and remains the same distance from the camcorder throughout the movement.

Uses for arcing

Arcing can also be used to unify two or more subjects. For instance, arcing in a semicircle round two people facing each other serves to unite them as a couple.

If you arc round a table at a dinner party, you not only show all the guests, you see them all in CU. This a much neater technique than panning from various positions or shooting a series of static shots.

Arcing round a group of subjects, such as a sports team, helps to emphasize their group identity rather than their individual identity.

1

2

Arcing round more than one subject not only unifies them as a group, but is a visually more interesting way of videoing them than shooting a static shot from one direction.

When the group has a definite front, you do not need to complete a full circle around them. Arcing through a semicircle or less – between 120° and 180° – is ideal.

To ensure the shot looks professional, keep the camcorder as steady as possible throughout the shot. Keep the subject central in the frame and maintain the same distance between it and the camcorder.

CRABBING

There is a special walk designed for arc shots called crabbing. To crab clockwise, face the front and bring your right leg in front of your left. The back of your right knee should touch the front of your left.

As your right foot touches the ground, your body weight transfers to it without any jolts. Bring your left leg round the back of your right and, as it touches the ground, slowly transfer your weight to it. Repeat this until you have finished the arc.

In professional videos, a good way of showing that a person is an outsider or newcomer to a particular group is to arc round the group and exclude the individual.

You don't have to move through the full 360° to get the effects of arcing. Many subjects have a definite front, so you don't gain much by shooting them from behind. In this case, arcing between 120° and 180° is the norm.

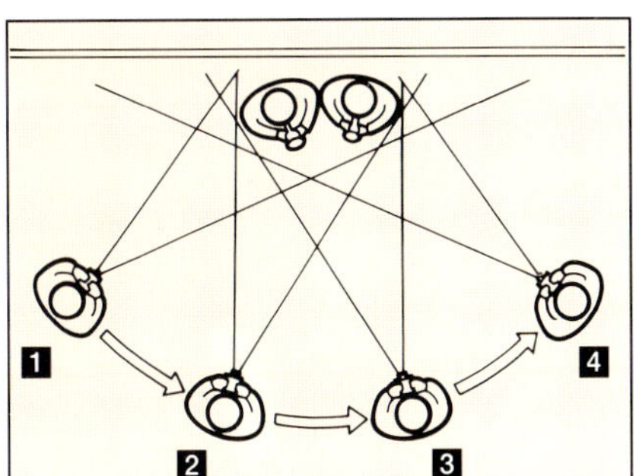

Shoot the Video

HOLIDAYS

"Holidays are one of the most popular subjects in video. Make sure you have all the accessories you need with you and pack them in a sturdy bag, so that you don't damage any equipment.

"Remember you're there to enjoy yourself, so don't try to video everything you see. Aim to produce a video that sums up the holiday location and includes any interesting places you visit."

"An essential shot in a holiday video is a good dramatic sunset. Be careful that the camcorder isn't fooled into setting the wrong white balance, though." (See *White Balance*, p. 52.)

"A good trick is to cut from inside a vehicle to a shot of it from the outside. You can even shoot a different tram – the viewer simply assumes it is the same one." (See *Logical Connections*, p. 89.)

"You have to be careful not to over-use the zoom lens – zooming in and out too much is called tromboning, and it can be irritating for whoever's watching your video.

"Here is a perfect example of when you should use a zoom lens. I started with an interesting subject containing action – the bather diving into the pool – and zoomed out to show the whole location." (See *Revealing a Scene*, p. 35.)

"Use the zoom lens to compose your subject while in pause mode. Only when you have the subject framed how you want it should you record." (See *The Zoom Lens*, p. 16.)

"Panning – sweeping the camcorder in a horizontal arc while recording – is the best way of showing a landscape too wide to capture with a static shot. When you can, always try to start and end on an interesting subject. Make the movement as smooth as possible." (See *Panning*, p. 28.)

"I always like to carry a variety of filters with me. These fit over the lens and alter the colour or appearance of the image.

"Here, I've used a starburst filter that turns points of lights – in this case, the evening sun – into a six-pointed star." (See *Starburst*, p. 57.)

"Every time you move to a new location when making your video, you should kick off with an establishing shot that shows the whole scene – so that the viewer knows where the action takes place. This wide shot shows both the hotel where we were staying and its setting." (See *Scene by Scene*, p. 76.)

"Another useful shot in video is the tilt. This is when you move the camcorder vertically up or down a subject while you are recording.

"To fit this church in the frame would have meant standing so far away from it that the detail would have been lost. Tilting enabled me to show the whole subject, while standing close." (See *Tilting*, p. 30.)

2
Recording an Image

Exposure
Focusing
Shutter Speed
White Balance
Colour Filters
Effects Filters
Lux Level
Add-on Lights
Lighting Problems
Two Lights
Four Lights

EXPOSURE

All camcorders can be set to fully automatic recording, but many allow some manual control. This enables you to record the scene in a different way from the camcorder's automatic settings. To make best use of these manual overrides, it is useful to know how an image is recorded.

When light passes through the lens, it registers an image on an electronic image-recording chip or CCD (charged-coupled device). This image is transferred to the viewfinder and tape, where it is permanently recorded.

How the iris works

The amount of light recorded by the CCD is known as the exposure. Between the lens and the CCD is a variable-sized opening called the iris. When the light is very strong, the iris narrows to reduce the amount of light. In dark conditions, the iris opens.

If the light level is even, the automatic exposure system easily works out the correct iris setting. But if you record a scene with very light and very dark areas, some camcorders may have difficulty. For instance, if you shoot a subject against a bright background, such as the sky, the camcorder narrows the iris because of the overall light level. This may render your subject too dark.

Backlight compensation

Most camcorders have a backlight compensation (BLC) button. When pressed, the iris opens by a set amount to let in more light.

If the camcorder has fully manual iris, you have greater control over exposure. Not only can you increase the exposure by the correct amount, you can also narrow it if you want an atmospheric silhouette.

The autoexposure system of some camcorders can be fooled by backlight situations into narrowing the iris. This renders the foreground subject too dark. By pressing the backlight compensation button or operating the manual iris, you can force the iris to open to brighten up the subject. Alternatively, recompose the scene, to give less contrast between the subject and background.

AUTOMATIC AND MANUAL EXPOSURE

Automatic exposure
If you are recording a pan, tilt, track or zoom, the light level may change during the shot. If you tilt down a tall building with a lot of sky at the start of the shot, the camcorder's iris opens and closes to compensate for the changing light level – pictures 1 2 3. This is not the desired result because the background light level is irrelevant. You want the subject to be exposed correctly.

Manual exposure
With manual iris – pictures 4 5 6 – you can do this. Zoom in on the subject and let the camcorder select the exposure value. Then select the manual iris option to switch off the autoexposure system.

FOCUSING

A wide-angle lens, a distant subject and a narrow iris create a scene where everything is in focus. Use this technique when the whole scene is the subject and you don't want to pick out anything in particular. This kind of shot is called deep focus.

A telephoto lens, a close subject and a fully open iris produce a shot with a very narrow depth of field. Use this technique when you want to isolate a particular subject from its surroundings. This kind of shot is know as shallow focus.

All camcorders incorporate an autofocus (AF) system. This chooses the most obvious subject, measures how far away it is, then moves the lens elements until the light rays from the subject converge on the CCD. The subject is then sharp.

When the subject is large, central and bright, the camcorder has no difficulty focusing. When the subject has no contrast or the light level is low, the focusing system might hunt around and ruin that part of the shot.

Some AF systems are cleverer than others. They lock on to a particular subject, so that if a person walks in front of the subject, the focusing system ignores them.

Depth of field

The lens can only focus on one point at a time. Some of the scene in front of and behind the subject is also sharp. This is known as the depth of field.

Three main factors determine the depth of field. First, the distance to the subject. The farther away the subject, the greater the depth of field.

Second is the focal length of the lens. Using the telephoto, the depth of field is narrower than with the wide-angle. That's one of the reasons why using the wide-angle while tracking is advisable, as there is less chance of the subject being out of focus.

The third factor is the size of the iris. When the iris is open, the depth of field is limited. In bright conditions, when the iris narrows, the depth of field increases.

You can manipulate these factors to create a wide or a narrow depth of field. These are known respectively as deep focus and shallow focus shots.

FOCUSING THROUGH BARS

Problems can occur when you attempt to shoot through glass or, as here, through the bars of a cage. The camcorder might focus on the bars instead of the subject.

To counter this, stand close to the cage and focus manually on the subject. The narrow depth of field throws the bars out of focus and reveals the subject.

CHANGING FOCUS

The viewer's eye is automatically drawn to the part of the scene that is in focus. A useful creative technique in video is to shift attention from one subject in a shot to another by moving the point of focus.

For this to work, the two subjects have to be at different distances from the camcorder. The depths of field also have to be narrow, so that when one of the subjects is in focus, the other is blurred.

Pulling and throwing focus

Practise the movement first. Mount the camcorder on a tripod and focus on the farther subject. Twist the focusing ring slowly, until the near subject is sharp. This is called pulling focus. Moving from the closer subject to the more distant one while recording is called throwing focus.

Uses of the technique

Pulling focus allows you to establish the location by focusing on the background, before pulling attention forward towards the main subjects of the shot.

Pull- and throw-focus shots are also used when new characters enter the scene. The lens refocuses on them.

SHUTTER SPEED

Every camcorder boasts a high-speed shutter, a term borrowed from still photography. (Still cameras have shutters that open to allow light to fall on the film.)

Camcorders don't have shutters, and they use a CCD instead of film. When the camcorder is switched on, light falls on the CCD continuously, but the CCD doesn't constantly record an image. Recording occurs only when the camcorder supplies the CCD with an electrical charge.

Camcorders take 50 or 60 snapshots a second. With 1/50 sec shutter speed, images can blur. This is only important for slow-motion playback and freezeframe.

Fields and frames

Like a television screen, the CCD is made up of a number of horizontal lines. In some countries this number is 625, in others 525 (see p.151). The camcorder only supplies a charge to half of these lines at a time. It alternates between supplying a charge to the odd- and even-number lines.

Each of these half-images recorded by the CCD is called a field. Two fields, one of odd-number lines and the other of even, are interlaced to form a frame. Each field is a snapshot of the action at a given moment. If the shots are played back fast enough, the brain sees a moving image.

Fields per second

In most countries where the television screens have 625 lines, the CCD records 50 fields per second. Where there are 525-line TVs, camcorders record 60 fields per second.

With a 1/50 sec shutter speed, each charge supplied to the odd or even lines lasts for 1/50 sec. The CCD records an image continuously, as 50 fields are recorded a second.

STANDARD-SPEED SHUTTERS

The shutter speed is the length of time an electrical charge is supplied to the CCD to enable it to record a single image. Depending on the television standard of the country, either 50 or 60 charges are supplied a second. With normal shutter speeds of 1/50 sec and 1/60 sec respectively, the CCD records continuously.

The CCD is made up of either 625 or 525 horizontal lines. Each charge is supplied to the odd-number lines and the even lines alternately. This means only half the CCD is recording at any one time. Each half-image is called a field. When the fields are interlaced on playback, the full image is called a frame.

By using a high-speed shutter, you can freeze each image so that it is blur-free.

With a high-speed shutter, such as 1/1000 sec, each charge is supplied for only 1/1000 sec. As there are still only 50 charges per second, there are gaps of 19/1000 sec between each field when no image is recorded.

When you play back a moving subject recorded with a high-speed shutter, these gaps cause it to move like someone under a strobe light.

With a high-speed shutter, each field is blur-free, because most subjects hardly move in so short a time. Played back in slow motion, each frame can be seen clearly. This is ideal for analysing action, such as your golf swing or tennis serve.

HIGH-SPEED SHUTTERS

The CCD only records 50 fields per second, so if you use a 1/1000 sec shutter speed, the CCD records nothing for the rest of each field.

When the image is transferred to tape, the same 1/1000 sec snapshot is repeated 20 times, making up the full 1/50 sec. This ensures there are no unrecorded sections of tape.

Fast shutters are used principally to analyse action on slow-motion playback. They can also be used to produce a narrow depth of field. With a high shutter speed, the CCD is exposed to light for less time. The camcorder is forced to open the iris to let in more light, which narrows the depth of field.

WHITE BALANCE

Different light sources produce different coloured light. Tungsten bulbs produce yellow light and tend to colour objects yellow. Cloudy days produce white light, but on bright cloudless days, white objects can take on a pale-blue cast.

Our brains have a very sophisticated colour balance system. Except in extreme circumstances, they are capable of ignoring colour casts and perceiving colours accurately.

AWB systems
A camcorder's automatic white balance (AWB) system is designed to do the same thing. It measures the colour cast of the dominant light source, then boosts the other colours in the video signal to compensate.

Basic AWB systems have only two colour balance settings: indoor and outdoor. The system may select the wrong setting, however, if the light source is unusual. For instance, sunsets are often closer to yellow-orange than to the normal blue-white outdoor setting. If the camcorder sees the light as indoor, it boosts the blues in the signal, causing the image to look washed out.

Manual settings
More sophisticated camcorders let you set indoor or outdoor white balance manually. Some offer fully manual white-balance setting. Here, the camcorder takes a colour cast reading off a white surface and sets the white balance accordingly.

COLOUR TEMPERATURE

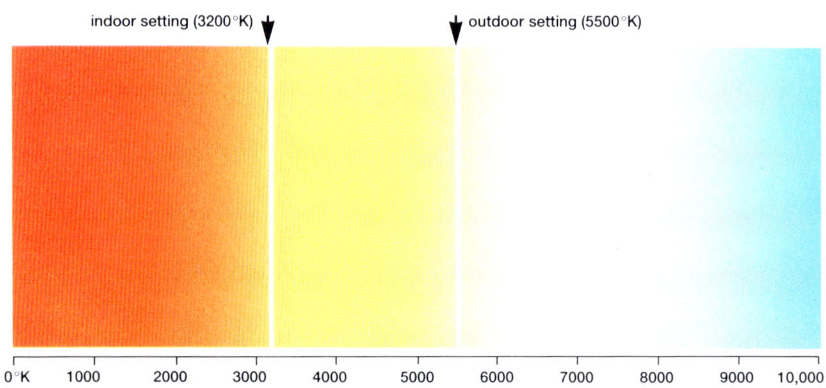

The colour of a light source is known as its colour temperature. It is measured in degrees Kelvin (°K). The two most common temperatures are 3200°K (tungsten bulbs) and 5500°K (summer sunlight). Sunrise and sunset are much closer to indoor than outdoor, at around 3500°K.

INDOOR

Tungsten lights give subjects a yellow colour cast. Your brain can filter this out, but a camcorder has to boost the blues to give an acceptably neutral result (*right*).

If you manually select the outdoor setting by mistake, the blues are not boosted. This can sometimes add to the intimacy of a scene (*above*).

OUTDOOR

On normal sunny days the colour temperature is around 5500 °K. If you mistakenly set the camcorder to its indoor position, the colours look very cold (*above*). You can sometimes use this effect to make warm sunny days look like bitter winter days, but generally it is best to select the outdoor setting (*right*).

COLOUR FILTERS

Colour filters are small pieces of transparent or semi-transparent plastic that either screw on to or fit over the front of your lens. This enables you to boost certain colours in the scene for creative effect.

(Most white-balance systems measure the colour cast through a sensor on the front of the camcorder, to prevent the AWB system compensating for the filter, and rendering it without effect.)

Warming and cooling filters

The simplest colour filters are warm-up and cooling filters. A faint amber or orange filter doesn't alter the image dramatically, but it does warm up skin tones, giving pale-skinned people a healthier glow and making cool scenes look warm and sunny.

Pale-blue filters have the opposite effect. They can make everyday scenes look cool and harsh. If you are shooting something dramatic, a pale-blue filter can add a sinister air.

Sepia filters

A frequently used filter is the sepia filter. Its brown tint is particularly associated with historical dramas. Sepia filters can also be used to reinforce the period feel of a location.

Watching a sepia-tinted video can get wearing, so use the effect sparingly. In drama, reserve sepia for flashbacks or for historical sequences.

Some of camcorders have sepia buttons. These record a sepia image without the use of a filter.

Sepia has become associated with the past through old black and white photographs, which faded to sepia. You can create a sepia effect by adding the appropriate filter to the front of your lens. Use the effect sparingly, however, as it can get wearing if it goes on for too long.

EXOTIC SUNSETS

If your camcorder boosts the blues when confronted by orange sunsets, you can counter this by using the appropriate filter. For a really dramatic sunset, use a deeper orange or even a red filter.

DAY FOR NIGHT

Blue filters are used to produce an effect known as day for night. Moonlit scenes can look very attractive, but visibility is severely limited in such low light. On sunny afternoons, however, there are no visibility problems.

You can convince viewers that they are seeing a moonlit scene by using a deep-blue filter. If you have manual control, underexpose slightly for an even more convincing effect. If not, try using a fast shutter speed, but beware of strobing.

Day for night works particularly well when the sun's rays are shining on water. With the blue filter, these rays look like streaks of moonlight.

EFFECTS FILTERS

Filters are used to alter the look of the scene being recorded. The most obvious are colour filters, but many other types are available.

Of these, the most basic are skylight and UV filters. These have very little effect on the video image, but when attached to the lens protect the front element from being marked or damaged. Some companies market dedicated protection filters.

Shallow-focus shots

If you need a shallow-focus shot and have manual control over the iris, you can open it to limit the depth of field, but this may lead to an overexposed image. Similarly, a high-speed shutter causes the iris to open wider, but there is a danger of strobing.

A better alternative is to use a neutral density (ND) filter. This simply reduces the amount of light passing through the lens. The camcorder's exposure system registers the scene as darker and opens the iris wider, reducing the depth of field.

Polarizing filters

The popular polarizing filter darkens blue skies, making them deeper and more appealing. It adds no colour cast, so white clouds remain white.

Polarizers can also eliminate harsh reflections. This makes them particularly useful in hot climates.

Polarizing filters can make a dramatic difference to your images. Skies look bluer and grass greener, but no colour cast is added. They also eliminate harsh reflections.

Polarizers have to have a specific orientation to work properly. If your camcorder rotates the filter when it focuses, the effect is lost. The answer is to set the camcorder on a tripod and hold the filter in front of the lens.

DIFFUSERS

Diffusion filters come in various strengths, from mild softeners to strong fog filters. They add a dreamy, romantic feel to shots of children or a wedding couple, for instance. This effect is called soft focus.

STARBURST

Starburst filters turn points of light into four- or six-pointed stars. This effect is most commonly used in pop videos, but it can also have its place in adding a fairytale quality to evening cityscapes.

LUX LEVEL

The intensity of light in a scene is measured in lux. Rooms lit by only a few candles might be no more than 10 lux, but the average living-room reads 100 lux or more. Extremely bright days might register as much as 100,000 lux and over.

Every camcorder boasts a minimum lux level. This is the amount of light the camcorder needs to resolve an image successfully. All camcorders have minimum lux levels of below 10, so the exact figure is not important.

The main problem with low light is that the camcorder has to increase the electric current to the CCD to boost the intensity of the video signal. This enables it to record an image, but the result is often grainy with washed-out colours. Increasing the current to the CCD is known as boosting the gain.

The other problem with low light is that some autofocus systems have difficulty focusing in such conditions. When this happens, just switch to manual focus.

Whenever possible, boost the amount of light inside by bringing in extra lights to the room.

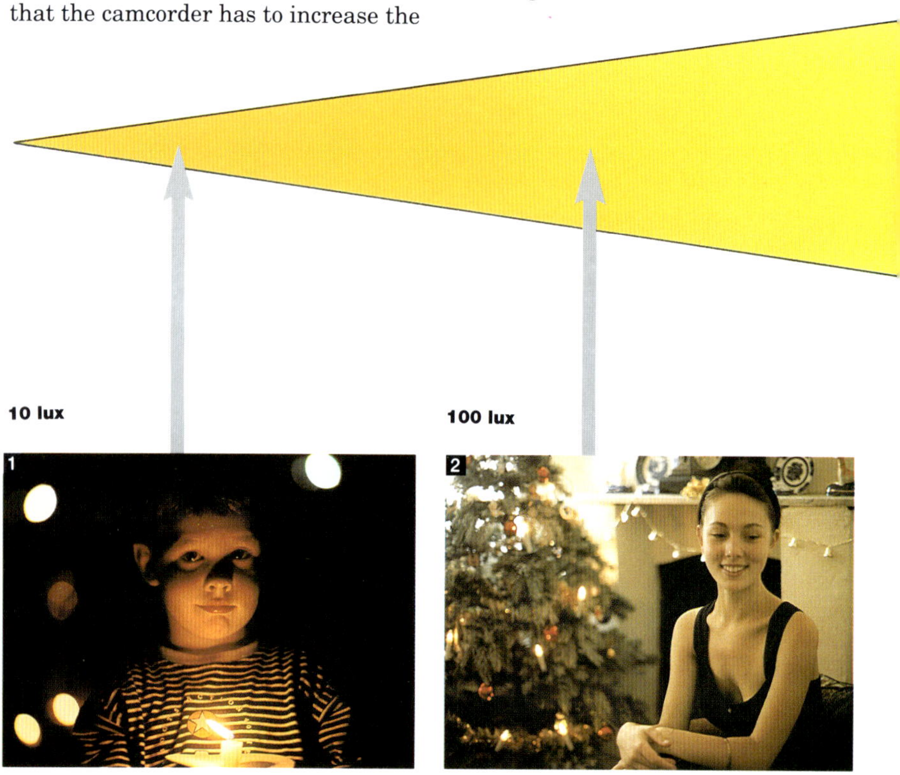

1000 lux

100,000 lux

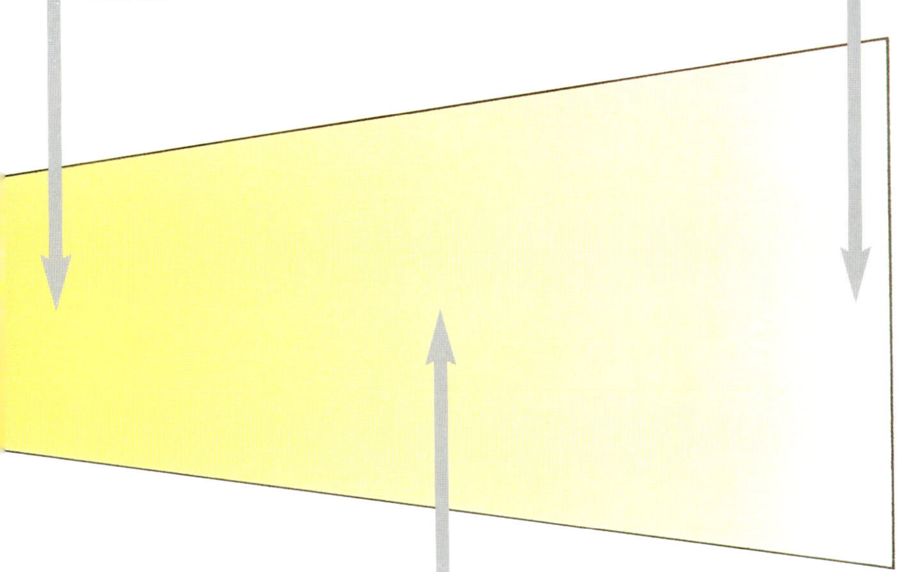

10,000 lux

1 Candle-lit scenes produce around 10 lux. You may lose the atmosphere if you try boosting the light.
2 An average room registers around 100 lux. Add extra lights if possible, removing shades from lamps that are out of shot.
3 Although dusk may produce around 1000 lux, the images can look grainy. Shoot at this time to get atmospheric shots.
4 Normal daylight gives around 10,000 lux. This is ideal for camcorders.
5 Extremely bright scenes can top 100,000 lux. A polarizing filter helps to eliminate reflections.

ADD-ON LIGHTS

Videos shot in low light can be colourless and grainy. To counter this, some camcorders come with clip-on video lights. These are powered by the camcorder's battery and throw out enough light to illuminate a fairly close subject. They normally have a low power output of around 20W.

More powerful camcorder-mounted lights are available with a outputs of 50–100W. These have their own rechargeable battery and are powerful enough to brighten an average room.

Bouncing powerful lights

With a fixed-output camcorder light you have to judge the best distance to stand from your subject to get the optimum results. If you stand too close, the light is too harsh and strong white areas (hot spots) appear on the image. These powerful lights also cast strong and unattractive shadows. The solution is to angle the light up so the light bounces off the ceiling. Even white ceilings warm up the light, but most AWB systems compensate.

Left: Using an add-on video light ensures enough light falls on the image to produce a good quality result. The problem with direct light is that, even when you are the optimum distance from the subject, the result is often harsh and flat.

Right: If you angle the video light up so the light bounces off the ceiling, you get a more even flood of illumination. This produces a much more attractive effect with no hot spots and no deep shadows.

REFLECTORS

Even when shooting in sunny conditions, you can improve your shots with a reflector. For close-ups, position the subject so the sun is to the side. Have someone else hold a reflector directing sunlight back at the face. Silver reflectors give a harsher reflection; gold reflectors add a warm glow.

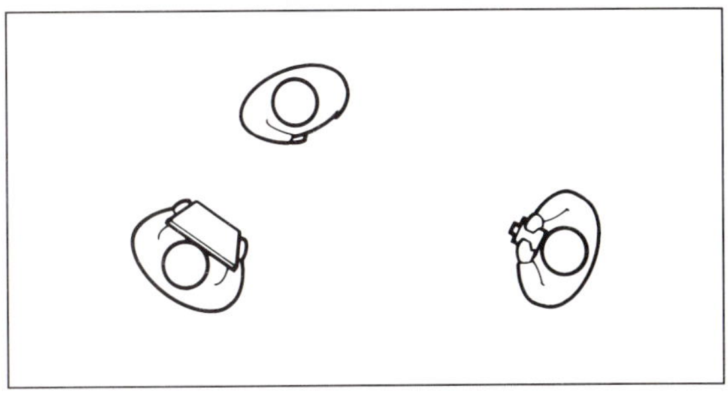

AVAILABLE LIGHTS

Camcorder-mounted video lights vary in power from as low as 10W to 100W. If you buy a light, consider the weight as well as the power output. If you have a palmcorder, try out the light first to make sure it doesn't overbalance the camcorder.

Lights are designed to slip neatly on to a camcorder's accessory shoe. If your camcorder doesn't have one, you can buy special brackets that clip between the camcorder and battery. The light can be attached to these.

LIGHTING PROBLEMS

Most camcorders can cope with one light source, but problems occur when there are two light sources with different colour temperatures. This is most common indoors, when there is a mixture of tungsten and window light.

This is known as mixed lighting. The camcorder chooses the brightest source and sets the appropriate white-balance setting. The areas lit by the other source are subject to a strong colour cast.

In these situations, try to boost one of the light sources and eliminate the other. If the tungsten light offers the greatest potential, draw any curtains and add extra video lights. If the windows are large, and it is a bright day, you may opt to eliminate the tungsten lighting. You don't have to turn all the video lights off, however. You can convert them to daylight.

Converting light sources

To do this, you need a sheet of blue gel. This is a small piece of blue perspex that can be bought from specialist camera and camcorder shops. When placed in front of a tungsten lamp it converts the colour temperature to daylight.

1

1 Backlight
Shooting indoors can create a number of lighting and colour balance problems. Positioning your subject by a window provides a lot of illumination. This gets round the need for the camcorder to boost the gain and produce a grainy image, but if the window is in the shot, the camcorder may register more light than is in the room and under-expose the scene. Not only is the subject rendered too dark, but if the scene outside the window is correctly exposed, it may draw the viewer's eye.

2

2 Compensation
The obvious solution to the backlight problem is to increase the exposure, either by opening the iris or pressing the backlight compensation button.

Boosting exposure provides only a partial solution, however. Although the viewer can make out more detail in the subject, the scene through the window becomes exceedingly bright, or burnt out.

As there is no direct illumination on the subject's face, there are no highlights and shadow to give the face detail. (Facial detail from lighting is called modelling.)

3 Reflector
A possible solution to the backlight problem is to use a reflector to bounce window light back on to the subject's face. You will need somebody to hold the reflector out of shot.

You can buy good reflectors fairly cheaply, but at a pinch you can make your own by rolling up a piece of aluminium foil then unrolling it so that it is slightly crinkled, and fixing it to a piece of card.

3

4

4 Add-on light
Instead of using a reflector, you can shine a video light directly on to the subject's face. Place the light to one side to give better modelling.

Although there is sufficient illumination, the white-balance system selects the outdoor window light setting, giving the subject a yellow cast.

5

5 Blue gel
The best solution is to place a blue gel in front of the video light. This produces even lighting on the face, while keeping a consistent colour balance. Because the subject is well-lit, the iris doesn't need to be open as wide as for the shots without the add-on light. This means the window light is not distractingly bright.

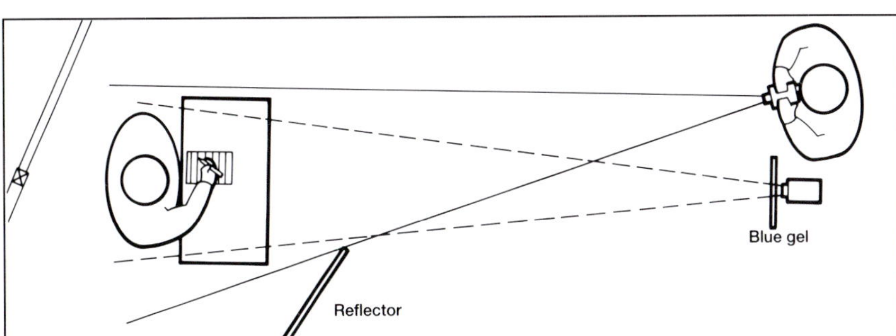

TWO LIGHTS

Lighting is not only to do with providing enough illumination for the camcorder's exposure system to produce a clear, brightly coloured image. With well-positioned lights you can create depth, conjure up a particular mood or draw the viewer's attention to details in the scene.

Lights can be described in terms of power output, colour temperature and whether they are hard or soft.

Hard and soft lights

A hard light is any strong point of light that casts a harsh shadow. Camcorder-mounted video lights are classed as hard, as are bare light bulbs and, of course, bright sunlight. Soft lights create few shadows, for instance, daylight on an overcast day.

Conventional lighting set-ups mix hard light and soft light. Hard lights can be turned into soft lights either by bouncing the light off a wall, ceiling or white umbrella, or by placing a diffuser in front of it.

A diffuser is any substance that lets the light through, but scatters the light waves, just as lampshades do to household light bulbs. Dedicated diffusers can be bought, but any thin white material will do.

Key and fill lights

The simplest lighting set-up is for lighting one person in CU or MS. It involves only two lights, one hard and one soft. The hard light is known as the key light, because it provides the primary illumination. The soft light is known as the fill light, because it fills in and softens the shadows created by the key light. This two-light set-up only works for non-moving subjects.

1 Key light
This should be hard and focused on the person's face. Placed next to the camcorder, it produces no shadows or attractive modelling on the face. Move the light 90° to the side, and the nose casts a deep shadow on the opposite cheek. The best position is between 25° and 45° to the side and between 10° and 45° above the level of the person's head.

STAND-ALONE LIGHTS

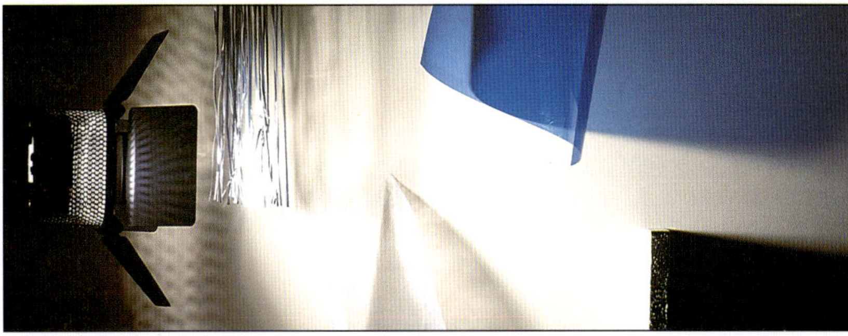

Stand-alone video lamps vary in power output from 100W to around 2000W. Up to around 300W, the lights are portable. Beyond that, they are best fixed in one position while being used. There are a number of attachments that can be added to the lights to vary the output.

- **Barn doors** Four metal shutters, often built in. They can be closed to narrow the light beam, creating a 'spotlight', or opened to create a 'floodlight'.
- **Flag** Any solid material, such as black card, placed in front of a light to alter the shape of its beam.
- **Snoot** Conical funnel often added to larger video lamps. Snoots produce a very narrow spotlight to illuminate a small area.
- **Cookie** A patterned screen through which light can pass to produce a mottled effect on a subject or background, making the light less harsh.
- **Diffuser** Anything that turns a hard light into a soft light. This can be a sheet of tracing paper or a specially designed diffuser placed in front of the light beam.

From left to right: 300W light fitted with barn doors; foil streamers used as a cookie; diffuser; blue gel; flag.

2 Fill light
This should be a soft light, less powerful than the key light and certainly not powerful enough to cast any shadows of its own. Place it on the opposite side of the face from the key light, around 30° to the side of the camcorder and lower down than the key. Monitor your lighting set-up through a TV if possible, moving the lights until you get the best result.

FOUR LIGHTS

You can successfully light your subject with only two lamps – the key and fill. But a third lamp is often added to improve the appearance of subjects and help pick them out from the background. This is the back light.

Back lights

The back light is a hard light with a very focused beam. When positioned directly behind a person, the back light creates an attractive halo around the head and shoulders. It can be positioned above, below or at the same height as the person's head, but you have to be careful that none of the light shines directly into the lens.

If the light is at the subject's head height, it is particularly important that the person doesn't move, otherwise the camcorder may be exposed to the light beam.

A more advanced lighting set-up for two people in MS can be achieved with the same number of lights. The two people have to turn slightly to the front, but still facing each other. A hard light is placed behind each of the subjects, acting as a back light.

If positioned correctly, the two lamps also act as key lights, shining over the shoulders farthest away from the camcorder, directly on to the other person's face. A soft fill light next to the camcorder lifts the shadows on the near sides of the faces.

Setting lights

The fourth important light is the setting light. This is used when you want to show detail in the background as well as the subject. The beam from the setting light should not fall on the subject, nor cast any deep shadows.

3 Back light
The back light picks out the subject from the background, but also creates an attractive halo around the person's head and shoulders. Unless you can guarantee the person won't move and expose the light, place the back light higher than the subject, between 25° and 60°. Don't place the light too high, as this creates a dark bib on the subject's chest.

FOUR-LIGHT SET-UP

The classic four-light set-up for a single subject.

1 The key light provides the principal source of illumination. It is placed above and to one side, to introduce shadow and modelling to the face.

2 The fill light is placed on the other side of the subject. It is a soft light that helps to lift the shadows, removing any harsh contrast.

3 The back light is placed behind the subject, creating an attractive halo that picks out the subject from the background.

4 The setting light, a soft light, is used to illuminate the background.

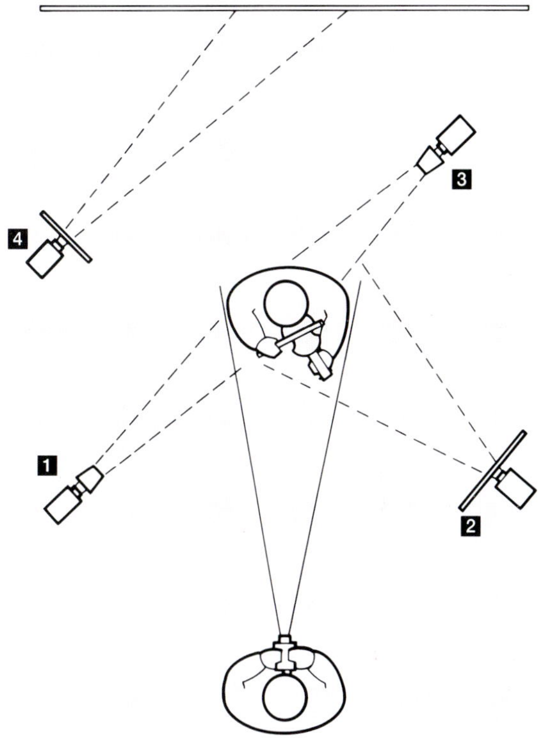

4 Setting light
The setting light is a soft light which illuminates the background. It should also eliminate any shadows cast from the subject by the key light. No part of the setting light should fall on the subject. If the background is plain and you want to make it more interesting, place a cookie or gel in front of the light to give a patterned background.

Shoot the Video

WEDDINGS

"You can guarantee that if you own a camcorder, you will be called upon at some time to video a wedding. If you are providing the official wedding video, you need to visit the church first to get the vicar's permission and perform lighting and sound tests.

"Remember to include as many of the guests as possible."

"If you know the bride well enough, pop round to her house to video her preparations – but don't get in the way. If you video young children, crouch so you are at their level." (See *Camera Angles*, p. 24.)

"You may be able to catch the bride-to-be sitting still while she is being made up. Mount the camcorder on a tripod, so you can concentrate on asking questions, without worrying about holding the camcorder steady." (See *Tripods*, p. 15.)

"The best position to stand during the ceremony is at the front of the church, to the side of the vicar. Preferably, use a directional off-camera microphone to record the sound." (See *Add-on Microphones*, p. 138.)

"If you can team up with a second person with a camcorder, get them to record the ceremony from the back of the church. Insert their shots as cutaways." (See *Insert Edit*, p. 112.)

"Zoom in on the bride and groom while they are saying their vows to add impact to the sequence." (See *Close-up*, p. 23.)

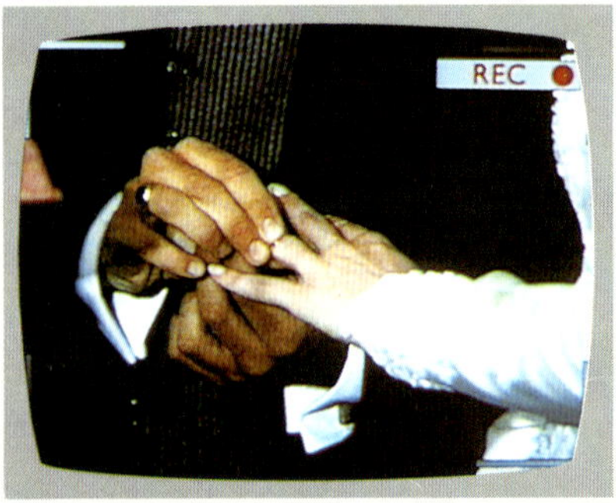

"Make sure you capture all the essential shots at the church. Zoom in to record a 'cut-in' of the ring being placed on the bride's finger, and get into position for the signing of the register."
(See *Cut-ins*, p. 87.)

"There is plenty of opportunity to video guests outside the church, while all the photographs are being taken. Shoot a montage of shots of as many guests as possible, to make sure everyone is included."
(See *Telling a Story*, p. 91.)

"Don't be afraid to crop in close on people, letting their faces fill the frame. But give them more room if they are moving, so they don't disappear off the side of the TV screen." (See *People*, p. 20.)

"A long shot of two people is not the ideal shape for a TV screen, which is wider than it is high. A good tip is to introduce an artificial frame, such as this doorway, which adds interest to the sides of the shot." (See *Frames Within Frames*, p. 27.)

3
Editing

In-camera Editing
Scene by Scene
Jump Cuts
The Line of Action
Sight Lines
Assemble Editing
Cutaways
Shot Suggestion
Telling a Story
Cutting on Action
Parallel Action

IN-CAMERA EDITING

The first two sections of this book are devoted to learning how to record individual shots. The second important area of video is editing. Very simply, editing is the process of deciding the length of each shot and the order in which to present them.

Two ways of editing

As you progress, you may wish to connect your camcorder to your video recorder and rearrange the shots into a different order. You can even buy additional pieces of equipment, such as edit controllers, which automate the process.

To begin with, it is easier to make all the editing decisions (length and order of shots) at the same time as making the shooting decisions (shot size, camera angle, shot type). This is called in-camera editing.

Since you make all the decisions as you go along, a video edited in-camera is finished as soon as you record the last shot. This makes it far more convenient than other, more advanced forms of editing.

Thinking in shots

If you intend to edit your home videos in-camera successfully, you need to learn how to think in shots. Don't simply press the record button and hope something interesting turns up, or your finished video may turn out messy and overlong.

Instead, decide exactly what you want to record, frame it, determine whether you want to hold a static shot or pan, and press the record button. When you pause, don't press the record button again until you have chosen the next subject and made all the shooting decisions.

The first discipline to learn when you are editing is to think in shots. Don't record everything you see. First determine the exact subject you want and make all the shooting decisions, such as which shot size, the best angle to shoot from, and what type of shot you think is appropriate. With fast moving subjects or quick-changing scenes, you may not have the time to consider every decision fully, but your ability to judge rapidly the best way of shooting a subject will improve with practice.

SHOT LENGTH AND BACKSPACING

How long should a shot last? The answer is 'about as long as a piece of string'. You won't necessarily know if your shot runs on for too long or whether it is too short until you view it on TV, but the more you shoot, the more adept you will become at judging the right length while recording.

As a general rule, moving shots can normally sustain interest longer than static shots. Static shots that contain moving subjects can be held longer than scenes without movement, and locations where there is no interesting sound or movement should last the shortest time, perhaps only two or three seconds.

For written subjects, hold the shot for as long as it might take a slow reader to read the written information.

Backspacing

One technical problem you have to face when determining how long to record a particular shot is backspacing. Every time you pause the camcorder, the tape automatically rolls back over the last second or so of the previous shot.

When you start recording again, the tape runs forward slightly. It does this for a technical reason that ensures there is a clean join between shots. If it didn't, distracting interference would appear on the screen at each edit point.

To allow for this, add a second or so to the start and end of every shot you record. This is particularly important if you are recording speech, as you might otherwise lose a few important words.

2

3

5

6

SCENE BY SCENE

When you think in shots, you don't record any subject until you have worked out the best way of shooting it and the length of each shot. This helps you to produce home movies that are far more watchable than videos where the operator has been a bit trigger-happy.

What makes good videos stand out over mediocre videos, though, is their structure. There is nothing wrong with a home movie that is simply a collection of well-composed subjects, but if you structure your video so that it tells a story, you will produce something that is far more likely to engage the viewer's interest.

Filming in scenes

The key is to think in scenes, as well as in shots. A scene is a collection of shots concerning the same subject, normally set in the same location.

If you were using a camcorder on holiday, you might plan your day so that you started with breakfast, spent the morning at the beach, visited a market in the afternoon and went to an open-air restaurant in the evening. If you wanted a record of all of these events, you should think of them and shoot them as four individual scenes, each one lasting perhaps only a minute or so.

Planning and structuring 20 1-minute movies is a lot easier than structuring one 20-minute movie. Each scene tells a story itself, and should progress the overall story.

ONE SHOT OR THREE?

To move from an LS to a CU, you can either dolly in or zoom in. A possible disadvantage with this approach is that

Establishing shots

At the start of each scene, you should let the viewer know that time has passed and the action has moved on. This means starting each scene with an establishing shot.

Establishing shots should instantly let the viewer know where the scene takes place. Long shots are often used for this, as they can show a wide location. But there is no reason why a close-up, such as a written sign, can not be used.

In the above scene, we start with an establishing shot **1** showing the beach and the lifeguards, and then move into the action. More shots could be included here, before we finally move to the closing shot **4** showing the whole beach.

At the end of the scene, use a closing shot to withdraw the viewer from the action. Hold the shot for 6 or 7 seconds, slightly longer than it deserves. The viewer's attention starts to wander, which helps distance them before starting the next scene.

the best shooting position or angle for the LS might not be the best direction to shoot from for a CU.

An alternative is to shoot three separate shots. This lets you choose the best shooting position and lens for each.

JUMP CUTS

When you pause the camcorder after a shot, then start recording a second shot, this is known as cutting. If we shoot one shot of a location and follow it by a shot of a person, we can say we have 'cut' from the location to the person.

Generally, you are free to cut from one subject to another as you like, but if you cut between two shots of the same subject within a scene, a special problem called a 'jump cut' can arise.

1

Filming a jump cut

Hold your camcorder steady and record a few seconds of somebody engaged in an activity such as washing a car. Pause the camcorder, but keep it to your eye. After about 10 seconds start recording again. Record for a little longer, then play back what you have shot. At the point where you cut between shots, you will find the person jumps slightly in the frame.

Although this technique is acceptable in pop videos, in more conventional productions it jolts the viewer. Like shaky camera work, it draws attention to the poor technique, and detracts from the video.

Indecisive and shock cuts

The best way of cutting between two shots of the same subject is to change the shot size and the angle you shoot from. If you change the shot size only slightly, you will create a jump cut known as an 'indecisive cut'.

Changing the shot size drastically, say from LS to CU, is known as a 'shock cut'. This can jolt the viewer, too; such extreme changes can be used to reinforce a dramatic moment.

Indecisive cut
When you cut between two shots of the same subject, make a definite change to the shot size or angle from which you shoot, otherwise you will create a jump cut. Between shots 1 and 2, the shot size changes only slightly, giving an indecisive cut. This will jolt the viewer when played back on TV.

Good cut
Make the size change count, as between shots 1 and 3, where we cut from LS to MS. Watch out that the subject doesn't move its head or change its stance between shots, as it can then still appear to jump in the frame, even if you change the shot size correctly.

Shock cut
Cutting between an LS and a CU, as between shots 1 and 4, can result in a shock cut, where the change is so strong it jolts the viewer. Unlike the indecisive cut, which simply looks wrong, the shock cut can act as a mild 'slap in the face' to draw the viewer's attention to the close-up.

THE LINE OF ACTION

Changing the shooting angle when recording a moving subject can cause problems. Try recording a shot of a subject travelling across the screen from left to right. When it has moved out of the frame, pause the camcorder, cross to the other side of it and record a second shot. This time it enters the frame from the right and exits to the left.

When you play the sequence back, notice how the subject appears to change direction between shots. It appears to be heading back to where it came from, even though it is still travelling in the same direction.

To avoid this confusion, film-makers use a simple device called the 'line of action'. Moving subjects create an imaginary line along the direction in which they are moving, extending in front of and behind them.

180° rule

From the line of action comes the '180° rule': if you record a moving subject from one side of the line, you should not record the next shot from the opposite side of the line.

If you want to move to the other side of the line, first shoot from the line itself, with the subject moving either towards you or away from you. This is known as a 'buffer shot'. From here you can move to either side of the line.

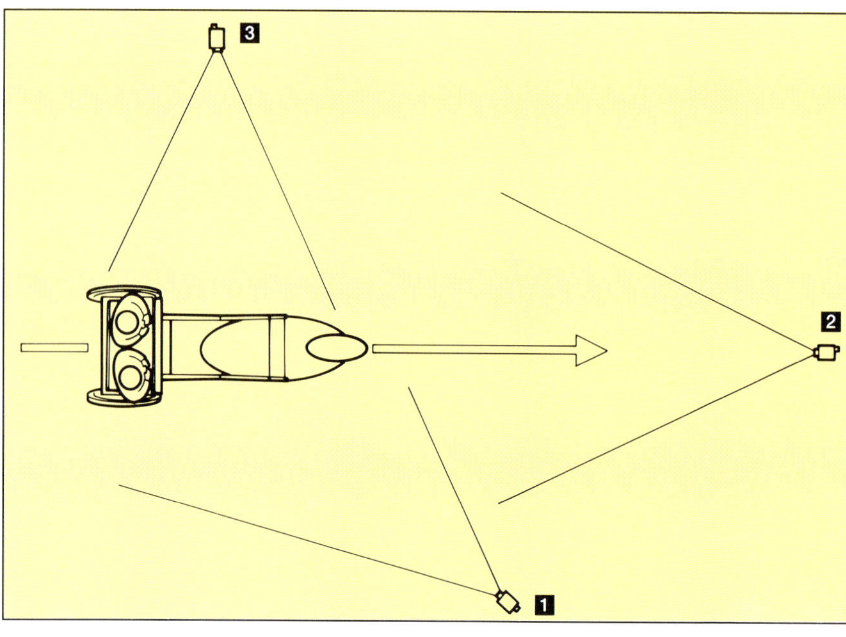

Moving subjects have screen direction. In shot 1, recorded from position 1 on the diagram, the subject moves from left to right. If we then cut to shot 3, recorded from position 3, the subject appears to have turned round.

One way of legitimately crossing from position 1 to position 3 is to separate them by a buffer shot from position 2, which is on the line itself. If shot 2 is inserted between shots 1 and 3, the confusion is removed.

SIGHT LINES

Moving subjects aren't the only things that generate a line of action. Anything with eyes also generates a 'sight line' in the direction it is facing. For instance, if you record a boy on a beach facing towards the left, then cut to a shot of him facing right, he appears to have turned round, even though he hasn't moved.

Such mistakes will not ruin a simple holiday video, but as soon as you attempt something slightly more ambitious, such as a documentary video or a rehearsed conversation, crossing sight lines will confuse the viewer, detracting from any serious point you are trying to make.

Filming conversations

The most common situations where sight lines come into play are two-person conversations, found in both drama and documentary interviews. When you have two people seated at a table, as here, you can record their entire conversation in mid shot from one position with the two people in the frame.

Visually, the scene is far more interesting if you cut between this

1

MOVING ACROSS THE SIGHT LINE

A shot of one of the people from the line itself (with the camcorder on the table) is called a point of view close-up. When the camcorder is placed here, the person looks directly into the lens. This is more likely to hold the viewer's attention than shooting the person in profile.

Shots taken from the sight line don't act as very good buffer shots. You can still potentially confuse the viewer if you cut from a point of view close up to a shot taken from the other side of the line.

Dollying

The simple way of moving from one side of the sight line to the other is to physically move the camcorder over the line. This involves dollying in a smooth arc around the table, using a dolly or a Steadicam JR.

A possible arc is shown on the diagram between positions 3 and 4. As there is no cutting, there is no chance of the viewer being disorientated by the move. Once you are at position 4, however, you have to stay on this side of the line if you cut to a different position. You can't cut from position 4 to position 1.

If the two people are not looking at each other, for instance if they are sitting side by side, the sight line still runs between them and not in the direction they are facing.

shot and close-ups of the two people. This allows you to observe the speakers' facial reactions in detail.

Re-establishing the scene

You don't always have to show the person speaking. If the listener's reaction is more interesting, show this instead. Cut back to the mid-shot position every so often to refresh the location in the viewer's mind. This is known as a 're-establishing shot'.

You will notice from the diagram that the sight line runs between the two people. Any shot from this side of the line is acceptable, but cross to the other side of the line and the woman appears to have moved to the other side of the table.

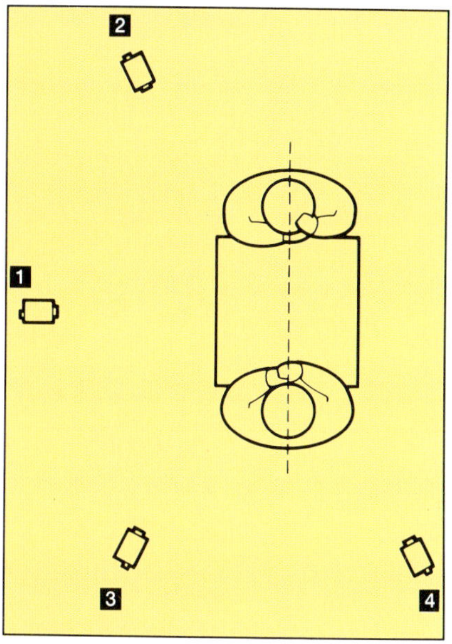

Conversations play an important part in video, from interviews to rehearsed speeches in drama. You need to observe the sight line running between the two people, or you may confuse the viewer and detract from the content.

Shot 1 is the establishing shot. From here, the viewer can see both people clearly. Shots 2 and 3 show the individual subjects. You can increase the shot size to draw attention to what is being said, and vary the camcorder's angle for over-the-shoulder shots.

Shot 4 is potentially confusing, so should not be used.

ASSEMBLE EDITING

One of the drawbacks of editing your home movies in-camera is that you only ever have the option of altering the portion of the video you recorded last. If you made a mistake earlier in the video, or decide you want to include a shot, it's difficult to do anything about it once you've recorded something else after it.

Problems with in-camera editing
No matter how careful you are, there are so many things that can go wrong. The most obvious oversight is thinking the camcorder is in pause mode when it is really in record mode. This can lead to long stretches of pavement appearing in the middle of your movies.

Other problems arise because the shots appear a lot shakier on the final video than you remember them, or because the autofocus system took longer to focus than you'd anticipated.

Similarly, you might be unaware that a juggernaut drove past just as somebody was saying something interesting to camera. All these mistakes find their way on to the finished tape.

Advantages of assemble editing
That's why most people who get seriously into video eventually realise

By treating all of your shots as building blocks, you are free to miss out any mistakes and rearrange your shots into a better order.

The top three pictures 1 2 and 3 show a series of shots as they were recorded. First the race is seen, next the winner is seen being led away, and finally a good establishing shot is recorded.

When assemble-editing the sequence, the establishing shot 3 is shown first and followed by shots 1 and 2 which were recorded earlier.

the limitations of in-camera editing and progress to assemble editing.

With assemble edit, every shot you record is simply a building block that may later be incorporated into your home movie. The finished video is produced on a tape in your video recorder by copying the good shots one by one from your camcorder.

Time for decisions

In many ways, assemble editing is easier than in-camera editing. If you are unsure whether to include a shot or not, you can simply record it and decide if you want to keep it later.

Similarly, you don't have to judge the duration of a shot when you shoot it. Instead, record it for slightly longer than normal and cut it down when you copy it to the video recorder.

Assemble editing allows you to make all of the important editing decisions at leisure instead of at the time of recording. As you are not under pressure, you are more likely to make the right decisions than when you are editing on the hoof.

Rearranging shots

Another advantage of assemble editing is that you can rearrange your shots. You might shoot some shots at an event and half way through spot a really good establishing shot. As you are rearranging the shots later, you can record it at any point on your camcorder tape and copy it over at the start of the scene when you edit.

As you get more proficient at editing, you will find there are other enhancements you can make, such as adding commentary, background music or special effects.

Disadvantages

The main disadvantage of assemble editing is that it is much more time-consuming than in-camera editing, as you still have a major task on your hands after you have finished shooting. However, you may find editing your video in this way is as enjoyable as shooting or watching it.

CUTAWAYS

You could describe a well-edited video as 'life without the boring bits'. The art of good editing lies in being able to condense time without making the video appear disjointed.

Eliminating chunks of dull action from your video is easy between scenes. If you end one scene of your video with an atmospheric red sunset, you can start the next with people going on a trip the following morning. The viewer accepts this condensation of time without question.

How jump cuts can happen

Within a scene, things are different. Because of the convention that has grown up in the movies, people expect that one shot occurs immediately after the previous one.

If we record a shot of a toddler at mealtime with her spoon in her food and cut to a shot where her spoon is in her mouth, there will be a jump cut, even if the shot size and shooting angle are changed correctly, because the spoon appears to jump when we don't expect time to have elapsed.

The greatest weapon editors have when it comes to condensing time is the 'cutaway'. A cutaway is a shot of any subject related to or occurring close to the main action, but not the main action itself.

Using the cutaway

If you record a sports match, every time you pause the camcorder there is a chance you will produce a jump cut, because the action will have moved on. The solution is to insert a cutaway between the two 'master shots' of the game. A suitable cutaway might be of someone in the crowd or a person walking past with a dog.

When you cut back to the game again, it doesn't matter if the action has moved on, because the viewer accepts that time passed. A 2-second cutaway can replace several minutes of missing action.

Like establishing shots, good cutaways can be recorded at any time. In fact, it is a good idea to build up a supply of useful cutaways, such as crowd shots.

CUT-INS

A cut-in is similar to a cutaway, but it is normally a close-up of the main subject, instead of something occurring near by. It is most often used by interviewers who want to miss out part of an interview or hide a shaky zoom. Nervous hand gestures are a favourite subject for a cut-in.

When you cut from shot 1 to shot 3 in this sequence showing a procession of carnival floats, the viewer will notice a jump cut because the action has moved on, although the shooting position is still the same and the viewer doesn't expect any time to have passed.

The answer is to insert a cutaway – a related shot taking place near the main action. This helps to 'plaster over the crack' so that no jump in the action is noticed. A short cutaway can replace minutes of main action.

SHOT SUGGESTION

We have seen how a movie convention has developed that, when the camcorder cuts between two shots in the same scene, the viewer subconsciously assumes that no time has elapsed.

Far from always being a problem, you can use people's tendency to make assumptions about what they are watching to help the flow of your video. You can also use it to cheat the viewer into making incorrect assumptions about a scene.

Tricking the viewer

Try setting up the camcorder on a tripod and pointing it at a friend. Get her to stand perfectly still with her hand out. Pause the camcorder and place something in her hand. Start recording again.

When this is played back, the viewer may be jolted for a fraction of a second after the object appears, but because the trick is not particularly subtle, all but the least sophisticated viewer will understand what has happened almost immediately.

More subtle tricks can be played when you cut between different subjects in the same scene. Because the brain is constantly trying to make sense of what it is seeing, it will make false connections. Three of these are known as spatial, temporal and logical connections.

SPATIAL CONNECTIONS

When cutting between two shots in the same scene, you need to let the viewer know how the first shot relates to the second shot spatially.

One method is 'cutting on the look'. Whenever you see a person looking in one direction, the assumption is that the next shot is what they see.

This can be used to trick the viewer. In one shot a person screams, in the next we see a snarling tiger – recorded at a different time, of course.

TEMPORAL CONNECTIONS

The brain has a tendency to assume that no time has elapsed between shots. This means you can shoot two similar actions from different perspectives and edit them together in such a way that they appear to be continuous action.

Use this when videoing a sport such as cricket or tennis. First, shoot a static shot of someone bowling or serving, then a static shot of the batsman or the other player hitting a different ball. Despite the camcorder having been paused, the two shots are seen as part of the same action. This looks a lot better than shooting a long shot or trying to pan.

LOGICAL CONNECTIONS

If you went on holiday, you could record a shot of a plane landing, then a shot of your family in the resort. The viewer assumes it is your plane, even though you couldn't possibly video the plane and be on it at the same time.

The most common 'cheat' establisher is showing the outside of a building and following it with a shot of people in a room. The viewer assumes the room is inside the building shown in the previous shot.

TELLING A STORY

Every shot you record can be described in two ways. The graphic description tells the subject, shot type, lens setting, camera angle, shot size and so on. The narrative description tells how the shot advances the story you are telling.

The narrative description needn't be complicated. Most shots in a straight record of an event simply show what happened next.

Similarly, a shot of an attractive or dramatic scene might be included because of its potential to inspire awe in the audience.

Interesting your audience

When you plan your videos, keep the audience in mind the whole time. Your aim should be to keep them interested. Even if every shot is perfectly clear, people's attention will soon wander if the subject doesn't engage their interest.

Make a point with each shot

When you assemble edit, it is worth making a note of what you think each shot adds to the story. This way, every shot has to fight for a place.

If you can't think of a good reason for including a shot, imagine how the video would look without it. If the video doesn't gain anything by its inclusion, consider missing it out.

A shot doesn't have to tell a story in the strict sense of the word. Cutaways advance the narrative, for instance, by condensing time and showing the viewer something interesting in the immediate environment.

The simplest way of keeping your audience interested is to present your story as a series of questions and answers. For instance, imagine you made a video of a trip to the zoo. In one shot you show an animal, and in the next you show people looking at it.

Now imagine you edited these shots in the opposite order. First you see people looking through the bars of a cage, then you cut to show what they are looking at.

This time, the first shot raises a question in the viewer's mind, 'what are the people looking at?'. When you show the animal first, no question is posed. By posing questions you stand more chance of engaging and keeping the viewer's interest.

Creating suspense

In many instances, narrative poses a question in one shot that is answered in the next. You can sometimes make your video more interesting by not answering the question straight away – this is called creating suspense.

For the suspense to work, however, the question has to be important

enough for it to stick in the viewer's mind. For example, if you watch a murder mystery on television, the central question, 'Who is the murderer?' is usually important enough to hold the viewer's attention for the whole movie.

With our shot of the people looking through the bars of a cage, however, if you don't answer the question straight away, the viewer is likely to forget all about it.

Montage sequences

A special kind of narrative where the shot order isn't important is the montage sequence. In a montage sequence, the intention is to convey an idea or a mood, or to sum up a character or location.

All kinds of ideas can be expressed by a montage sequence. By showing a handful of 3- or 4-second shots, you can give an impression of concepts like enjoyment, beauty or poverty.

All of these shots were recorded at a Chinese garden. What makes this kind of sequence (a montage sequence) different from normal forms of storytelling is that the order in which the shots appear isn't important. The intention is simply to give an overall impression of the garden's tranquillity.

Each shot adds to the atmosphere and reinforces the restful quality of the scene. None of the shots needs appear on the screen for more than 4 or 5 seconds.

CUTTING ON ACTION

Many people who use their camcorder a lot eventually get frustrated at having to record events as they unfold. With the video-maker's eye, you can often see how to improve the video if you could only step in and direct the action a little.

In many kinds of video you can. Short documentaries and even dramas are within your reach if you are a member of a video club or your family or circle of friends is willing to get involved.

As soon as you start to direct the action, you can reshoot shots, or even whole scenes, if you don't like the way they look. You also have access to more advanced shooting and editing techniques that help the flow of your video.

One such technique is 'cutting on action'. It is designed to help prevent jump cuts when you cut between two shots of the same subject.

A1

A2

Shooting twice

For cutting on action, you have to shoot the same action twice, once from the camera position you want for the first shot, and then from the camera

B1

B2

position of the second. When you assemble edit, you start the second shot at the exact point that the first shot ends.

Finding the right point to cut
In theory, you can choose any point in the action, but in practice there are better edit points than others. Cutting on action relies on the important notion that slight differences in the

A4

A3

B3

B4

position of the subject between shots, which would normally lead to a jump cut, won't be noticed if the edit point comes in the middle of an action.

Cutting on the turn
The simplest example of cutting on action is called cutting on the turn – particularly useful when the subject is talking to camera

In the first shot, the woman faces the camcorder. At a natural pause in her speech, she turns through 90° and the camcorder cuts. The second shot starts with her in profile. After you start recording, the woman rotates through 90° again and continues to talk. Edit the shots so the cut occurs during the turn.

Pictures A1 to A4 represent the first shot, B1 to B4 the second. When you cut in the middle of an action – A3 to B3 – the movement hides potential jump cuts. When cutting on the turn, the woman has to remember only a few sentences before turning. She can then prepare for the next bit of commentary and record that. You can turn a number of times in the same speech.

1

2

PARALLEL ACTION

We have seen how you can help structure your home movie by dividing it into scenes. In most cases, one scene ends before another begins, but this needn't be the case.

Once you take control of the action, you can rearrange your shots so that two scenes are intercut. A shot from one scene is followed by a shot from another, then back to the original scene. This technique is known as 'parallel action'.

Many parallel action sequences show two events taking place at the same time, but in different locations. Often the two scenes eventually come together.

Car chases in adventure movies are good examples of parallel action, as are those scenes in crime thrillers where the action cuts between a villain robbing a safe and a security guard doing the rounds.

In both cases, there is a great deal of suspense in the sequence, arising from the viewer trying to guess whether the two scenes will eventually come together, and what the outcome will be if they do.

Condensing time

Parallel action sequences also allow you to condense time. As you are cutting between two separate pieces of

5

6

action, you can miss out whole chunks every time you cut back to a scene.

In effect, the shots from one scene serve as cutaways for the shots from the other scene. And vice versa.

Creating a story

The sequence here shows a very simple example of parallel action. The woman is waiting to catch a train, and the man is trying to catch up with her before she goes, presumably to try and stop her.

You can always trick the viewer by giving a completely false ending. Despite the assumption behind the sequence on these pages that the man was chasing after the woman, there is no reason why the couple even have to know each other. The flowers could have been intended for someone completely different.

Parallel action sequences are also useful when contrasting or comparing two subjects. You could, for instance, cut between two methods of performing a task (traditional and modern) or between a family picnic and animals feeding at a zoo.

A lot of boring activity has been missed out between shots 1 and 3 and shots 3 and 5, but the viewer doesn't notice the jumps because shots 2 and 4 from the second scene serve the same purpose as cutaways, helping to plaster over the gaps.

There is suspense in the scene until shot 7, when the man catches up with the woman. In shot 8, we see that the flowers have been battered in the mad rush, and realize the meeting is perhaps not as romantic as it might have been.

Shoot the Video

CHILDREN

" 'Never work with children and animals', the saying goes. But I did just that the day I took my camcorder to the funfair and the zoo. And we all had a really wonderful time.

"As with taking your camcorder on holiday, don't let it spoil your fun. Always have it at the ready to record a good shot, but remember you're supposed to be enjoying the day out too."

"To start the day, we took a ride on an old steam engine. I wanted to show the train arriving, followed by the children getting on it. By editing in a cutaway of a sign between the two shots, I managed to miss out some of the action, without the cut jolting the viewer."
(See *Cutaways*, p. 86.)

"I could have recorded this simple sequence in one shot. However, this would have involved having to pan rapidly, and may have looked messy. I first videoed the ball being thrown, then moved to a different position to watch it hitting the can. Although two throws were involved, the viewer believes the two shots are from the same throw." (See *Temporal Connections*, p. 89.)

"Crop in close for the reaction shot. The more the person faces the front, the greater the impact." (See *Viewer–Subject Intimacy*, p. 20.)

"Some camcorders have a macro mode that lets you crop in tightly on tiny subjects." (See *Close-up*, p. 23.)

"An interesting technique in video is to cut between two subjects for comparison – in this case between an otter and a person eating." (See *Parallel Action*, p. 95.)

"When shooting children, record from their head height. For these shots, I had to kneel on the ground to get low enough." (See *Camera Angles*, p. 24.)

"When cutting between two shots of the same subject, make the change in shot size quite large, otherwise you run the risk of producing a jump cut." (See *Jump Cuts*, p. 78.)

BAIRD
NICAM
STEREO
ARCHIV
nicam digital stereo
TOP TEXT PROGRAMMING
GRUNDIG
GV 280 S

4

Editing and Enhancing Equipment

Learning to Edit
Video Recorders
Synchro Editing
Edit Controllers
Time Coding
Insert Edit
Processors
Fades
Dissolves
Titling
Title Cards
Computer Video
Time Lapse

LEARNING TO EDIT

Assemble editing involves copying the shots you want to keep from your camcorder tape to a video recorder (VCR) tape. You also need a TV to monitor the editing process.

How to assemble edit
Connect the camcorder to the VCR and the VCR to the TV, using one of the methods described in the box below. When the VCR is in PLAY or PLAY/PAUSE mode, the image from the VCR tape is shown on the TV. When the VCR tape is set to RECORD or RECORD/PAUSE, and the camcorder is set to PLAY or PLAY/PAUSE, the camcorder image is shown on the TV.

To copy a shot, pause the camcorder tape at the start of the first shot and pause the VCR tape where you want to start recording. Release both pause buttons at the same time. At the point you want the shot to end, press the VCR's pause button. Cue the camcorder tape to the correct point for the start of the second shot and repeat the procedure.

Backspacing
Most VCRs have backspacing facility, which means that when you pause the VCR, the tape rolls back slightly to ensure a clean edit point. This means the last half a second or so of the previous shot is recorded over. Furthermore, the VCR doesn't start recording for half a second, so the start of the next shot is not recorded.

To overcome this, don't pause the VCR until just after the point where you want the shot to end. You should also pause the camcorder tape half a second or so before you want each shot to start.

THE RIGHT CONNECTION

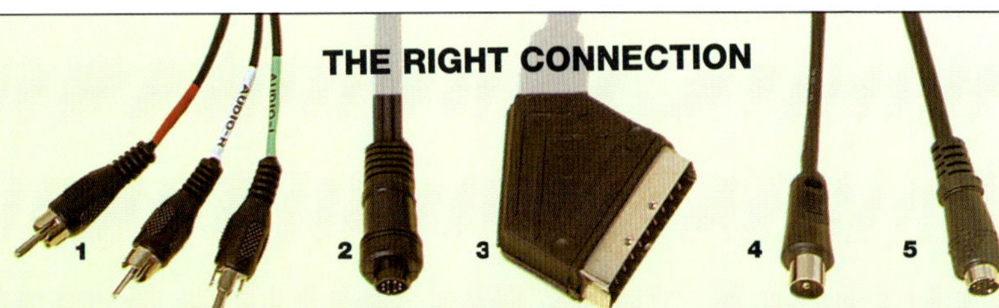

Camcorders come supplied with A/V leads, usually phono (1) or 8-pin (2). These carry the sound and picture signal to the VCR. If your camcorder uses phono leads and is mono, it has an output for video and an output for audio. If it is stereo it has two outputs for audio.

The A/V inputs on most VCRs take either phono or SCART (3) plugs. For SCART (also called Peritel or Euroconnector) you need to buy an additional lead.

If your VCR has no A/V input, you can connect the camcorder to the VCR's aerial socket using an RF-adaptor and aerial lead (4). This lowers quality and renders stereo sound as mono.

Super VHS and Hi8 camcorders have an S-output, which carries the high quality video signal. S-connectors (5) can be connected to a SCART socket or S-input.

HOW TO ASSEMBLE EDIT

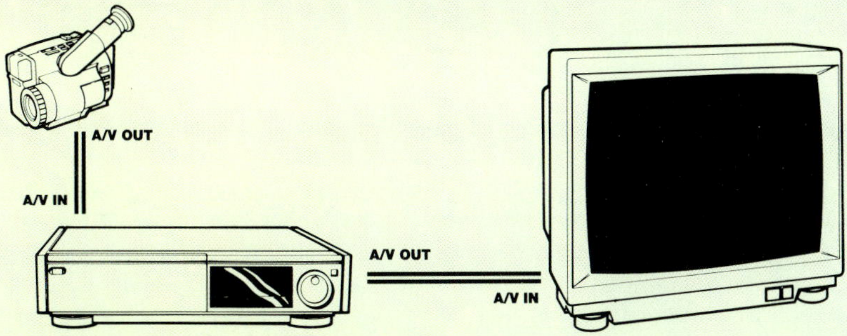

1. MAKE A LIST OF GOOD SHOTS AND THEIR COUNTER NUMBERS
2. PLAY/PAUSE CAMCORDER HALF A SECOND BEFORE START OF FIRST SHOT
3. ADVANCE VCR TAPE A FEW SECONDS AND SET TO RECORD/PAUSE
4. RELEASE BOTH PAUSE BUTTONS AT THE SAME TIME
5. RECORD FOR A FEW SECONDS AFTER END OF SHOT AND STOP
6. REWIND VCR TAPE AND REVIEW SHOT. WAS IT SUCCESSFUL?
   - NO → RECUE CAMCORDER AND VCR TAPES AND PAUSE BOTH → RELEASE BOTH PAUSE BUTTONS AT THE SAME TIME
   - YES → WAS THAT THE LAST SHOT?
7. WAS THAT THE LAST SHOT?
   - NO → CUE BOTH TAPES FOR NEXT SHOT AND RELEASE PAUSE BUTTONS → RECORD FOR A FEW SECONDS AFTER END OF SHOT AND STOP
   - YES → END

Before you assemble edit, make a list of the shots you want to copy, noting down the counter number at the start and end of each.

Keep a log book of all your good shots – even the ones you don't use straight away. You might find a place for them in another video.

VIDEO RECORDERS

People invest a lot of thought in buying a camcorder, but when you assemble edit, the VCR is equally important. Some VCRs are definitely better than others.

Important connections

The first thing to make sure is that it has all the right connections. Most new models have 21-pin SCART sockets. A lot of models designed with camcorder enthusiasts in mind also have phono leads. These are normally positioned on the front of the video, so you can connect your camcorder to the VCR without hassle.

Every time you copy from one tape to another, you lose some of the picture quality. If you own a hi-band camcorder (S-VHS, S-VHS-C or Hi8) you benefit from increased quality. You can retain far more quality if you assemble edit on to a Super VHS VCR rather than a standard VHS. Hi8 models are available, too.

Sound recording is also important. If you have a stereo camcorder, look for a hi-fi stereo VCR.

A number of other features are particularly useful for editing home movies, particularly a jog/shuttle, insert edit facility and audio dub.

USEFUL VIDEO RECORDER FEATURES

Super VHS is a better-quality format than VHS. If you have a hi-band camcorder, consider buying a hi-band VCR. Connect the camcorder to the VCR with an S-lead.

Hi-fi stereo reproduces sound far more faithfully than mono. If you have a hi-fi camcorder with a stereo microphone, look out for a hi-fi stereo VCR.

Audio dub enables you to rerecord the sound without recording over the picture. With a mono VCR, the original sound is lost. A stereo VCR gives you the option of mixing the old sound with the new.

Insert edit enables you to record over the picture part of your home movie, while leaving the original sound intact. With hi-fi stereo VCRs, you have the option of adding new sound to existing sound.

Jog/shuttle is one of the most useful devices for the serious editor. It enables you to move the VCR tape backwards or forwards in slow motion or frame at a time, so you can locate the edit points easily.

USING JOG/SHUTTLE FOR SLOW MOTION

Some highly dramatic moments may last for only a short time. To draw attention to the skill involved or to increase the dramatic impact, you may wish to show the action in slow motion.

Slow-motion shots are particularly suited to sporting events, such as athletics. In professional movies, they are often used for fight or dramatic action sequences.

Slow-motion shots
To perform a slow-motion shot, you need either a camcorder with high-quality slow-motion playback or two VCRs – one with jog/shuttle.

The scene should be recorded by your camcorder in the normal way. If the camcorder has slow-motion playback, you simply use this while the VCR is recording at the normal speed.

Using the jog/shuttle
If you don't have a camcorder with slow playback, record the shot on to a VCR with jog/shuttle. Connect the A/V output of this VCR to the A/V input of another VCR.

Use the jog/shuttle to play back the shot in slow motion, while recording with the second VCR.

Keeping quality
As you have to copy a copy of the shot, you lose even more quality than when you assemble edit normally. This is where using hi-band equipment is important.

SYNCHRO EDITING

Video recorders backspace the tape to ensure a clean edit when you press the PAUSE button. Backspace time varies from machine to machine, from a few frames to two or more seconds. Add the possibility of not hitting the two PAUSE buttons at the same time, and you introduce plenty of room for error.

To overcome this problem, manufacturers have developed ways of making editing more accurate. The simplest is synchro editing.

For this, all you need is a synchro edit lead and a camcorder and VCR with matching synchro edit sockets. When the lead is attached, you only need to press the PAUSE button on the VCR, and this will release the PAUSE button on the camcorder. It delays the camcorder to compensate for the backspace time.

SYNCHRO EDIT

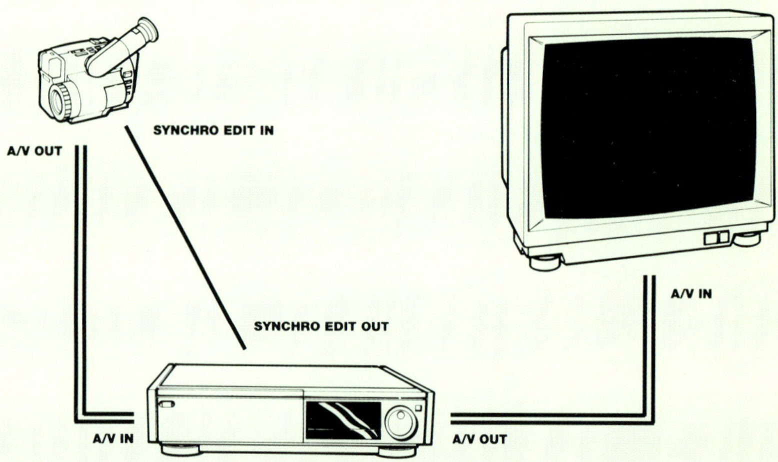

When you join the camcorder to the VCR for synchro editing, the A/V leads are connected in the usual way. However, a synchro edit lead is added to the set-up.

Synchro edit leads cost little more than a couple of camcorder tapes. Their disadvantage is that both the units have to be made by the same manufacturer, and they have to have synchro edit sockets.

Manufacturers know the backspace time of their machines, so they can build an accurate delay into the leads.

If you have a camcorder with synchro edit and want to buy an editing VCR, consider getting a model from the same manufacturer with synchro edit facility.

DOUBLE IMAGES

When the VCR is in PLAY mode, the TV shows what is on the VCR tape. When it is in RECORD mode, you see what is on the camcorder tape. Some people use two TVs – one permanently displaying the camcorder output. There are three ways of connecting this to your system:

1 If you have a hi-band camcorder, it has two outputs (S-connector and A/V). Feed one to the VCR and one to a monitor.

2 If you have a TV with two SCARTs, run the camcorder output to one of them and run an output lead from the second SCART to the VCR.

3 If neither applies, you need an A/V splitter. This takes an input from the camcorder and outputs two signals, one to the VCR and the other to the second monitor. This set-up is shown in the diagram below.

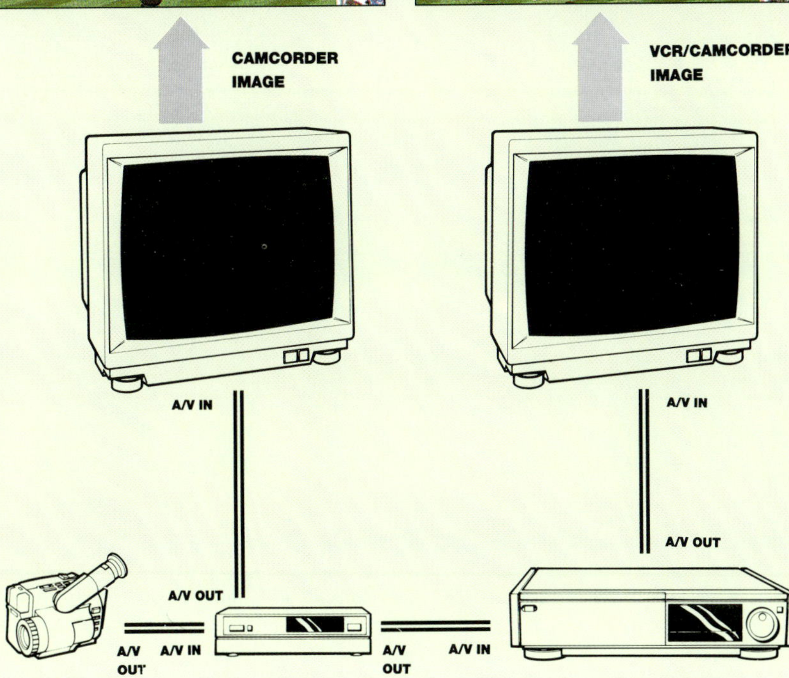

EDIT CONTROLLERS

Before you start assemble editing your video, make a list of all the shots you want copied to the finished tape and where to find them.

Once you have made the list, you have to determine the order in which you want to copy them. If there are only a couple of dozen shots, this is easy, but if there are a couple of hundred or more from your holiday, it can be a complex task.

Arranging the shots

Some people write a brief description of each of the usable shots on individual index cards. These can then be arranged in the appropriate order, and any excess discarded.

Once you have arranged them in this way, the main part of the creative process is over. The next task is the mechanical and time-consuming one of fast forwarding and rewinding to the start of each shot and copying the shots one by one.

Automation

Fortunately, the whole assemble-editing process has been automated by edit controllers. These vary widely in price and sophistication, but they all work in roughly the same way.

Just like camcorders and VCRs, edit controllers feature a set of transport keys (PLAY, RECORD, REWIND, etc.). When the edit controller is connected to your system, it can control both units, so you don't have to touch your VCR or camcorder except to change tapes. You still have

CONTINUITY OF APPEARANCE

When you are recording a lot of shots in a scene from various angles, it often makes sense to shoot all the shots from one angle, then the shots from another, and assemble edit them into the right order later, when you've finished shooting.

This can lead to another kind of

EDIT CONTROL SET-UP

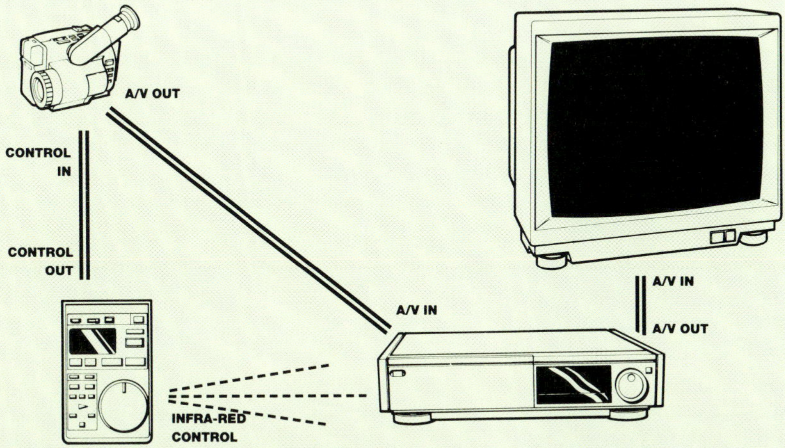

Most 'counter reading' editors send control signals to the VCR by infra-red remote control. But as they need to read the counter number on the camcorder to control it accurately, this information has to be sent down a wire.

Most editors use a lead that plugs into a socket on the camcorder. With 8 mm, this is normally the Control-L (also called LANC) socket, and with VHS it takes the form of a five-pin mini-plug.

jump cut, known as a continuity error. Always look out for glasses that mysteriously fill up between shots or limbs that appear to jump.

to fast forward to the start of each shot, but instead of starting to record, you simply press a 'store' button, and the edit controller remembers the tape position at that point. Forward to the end of the shot and store this position too.

Some controllers can store dozens of edit points, others only a handful. Once you have programmed in either to the capacity of the machine or as many as you want, press the auto-assemble control. You can then leave the machine to copy all the shots.

Basic edit controllers work by counting electronic pulses that are generated once a second by the camcorder. More sophisticated units read a 'time code'.

TIME CODING

Although edit controllers can save a lot of button-pressing by automating the assemble editing process, the pulse-counting models don't guarantee any more accuracy than editing manually. This is because they select the edit points by counting the number of pulses given out by the camcorder's tape counter (one a second) as it rewinds and fast forwards. Furthermore, it is possible for the tape to slip in the mechanism, and any errors will show up as inaccurate edit points.

Advantages of time coding

If the timing of your edit points is important, you need a much greater degree of accuracy. The system that has been developed to provide this is called 'time coding'.

Time code edit controllers work in the same way as pulse-counting editors. The difference is that they use a far more accurate system to remember the edit points.

Frame accuracy

With time code, each frame has a unique label that describes how many hours, minutes, seconds and frames it is into the tape. This label is invisibly 'written' on to the tape itself, so that no matter how inaccurate the transport mechanism, each individual frame can still be identified.

The two time code systems are the 8 mm version RCTC ('arctic') and the VHS system VITC ('vitsee'). Both can be written at the time of recording (if you have a camcorder capable of writing the time code), but only RCTC can be added to a tape once recorded.

VITC can be added to material only when it is being copied to another tape. This means you have to copy the whole tape once before you begin to assemble edit.

Time code is especially important for cutting on action. When you cut between two shots of the same subject, the neatest cut occurs in the middle of an action.

In the above sequence, the cut comes after the girl begins to raise her glass. It is timed so the glass is at the same point at the end of the first shot as it

TIME CODE SET-UP

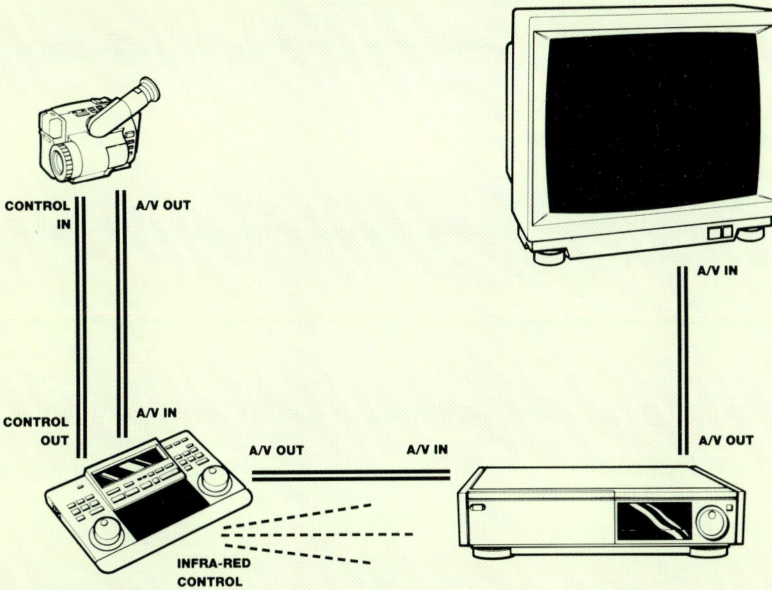

Time code editors are more expensive than pulse-counting editors, but are far more accurate.

With RCTC, the time code information is sent down the Control-L lead. With VITC, the information comes from the tape, so the A/V leads have to pass through the edit controller.

With most units, you are given the choice of controlling the VCR by infra-red or with leads. Infra-red does not guarantee frame accuracy.

is at the beginning of the second.

If you are not using time code, the end of the first shot might not match up with the start of the second. When the first shot overruns and you see part of the action twice, this is known as double action. When the first shot ends too soon or the second starts too late, this is missing action.

INSERT EDIT

In-camera editing and assemble editing are adequate when the sound for each of the shots is self-contained. But when you record a scene with continuous sound, such as live music, you have to record the whole scene in one shot. If you don't there will be the sound equivalent of a jump cut at every edit point. The solution is to use a third editing technique known as insert edit.

Not all camcorders and VCRs can insert edit. No 8 mm camcorder can, because of the way the system is designed. Some companies refer to the feature as video insert.

How to insert edit

With insert edit, you first record a shot, then record a second shot over a portion of it. Instead of pressing the RECORD button on your camcorder or VCR, you press the machine's INSERT EDIT button to record the second shot.

When you insert edit a shot, the camcorder or VCR records only the new picture over the first shot. It leaves the soundtrack from the original intact.

How insert edit works

VHS hi-fi stereo camcorders and VCRs record sound in three separate places on the tape. These are known as tracks. Left and right hi-fi tracks are recorded in with the video signal, and a mono track is recorded on the edge of the tape.

When you insert edit, you record over the video and the hi-fi stereo tracks, but the mono is left untouched. Most machines give you the option of recording new sound with the inserts, to add to the original, or recording no new sound with the video inserts.

Insert edit enables you to record cutaways or to change position without creating sound jumps. A 30-second shot of this band was

VIDEO	ORIGINAL PICTURE		NEW PICTURE
HI-FI	MUSIC		NO SOUND
MONO	MUSIC		MUSIC

HOW TO INSERT EDIT

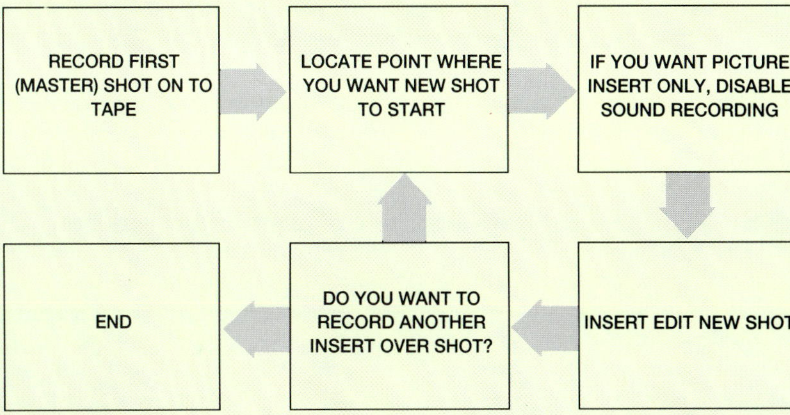

If your camcorder has insert edit, simply record the master shot for as long as you want. Then decide where you want the first insert. When you have located the position on the tape, press INSERT EDIT/ PAUSE and frame the cutaway.

The camcorder may give you the option of recording picture only. If it doesn't, plug an add-on mic – make sure it is turned off – into the external mic socket to disable the sound and press INSERT EDIT/PAUSE.

Insert editing on to a VCR is performed in the same way. Copy the master shot on to the VCR tape and rewind to where you want the insert to start. Find a suitable cutaway and insert edit. Don't connect the audio leads if you want to copy the picture only. The mechanism ensures the edit points are clean.

recorded. The music was recorded on to all three audio tracks. Cutaways were inserted into the shot using the insert edit facility. No sound was recorded on the hi-fi tracks, but the music remains intact and continuous on the mono track.

ORIGINAL PICTURE	**NEW PICTURE**
MUSIC	**NO SOUND**
MUSIC	**MUSIC**

PROCESSORS

If you are not happy with the picture quality of parts of your video, you may be able to improve the images during editing by passing the signal through a video processor. This gives you the option of altering part or all of the image. The most basic processors offer only functions that enhance or alter the signal, while more advanced models incorporate special effects and sound enhancements.

Basic features

- **Contrast** Allows you to strengthen weak images or soften over-contrasty pictures. Similar to the TV control.
- **Sharpness** When you copy from one tape to another, the quality is reduced slightly and the edges of a subject can blur. Increasing the sharpness reduces this.
- **Noise reduction** Cuts down the amount of interference on the image.
- **Brightness** Boosts the signal, particularly brightening the whites.
- **White-balance correction** Allows you to alter the relative intensities of different colours in the signal. Useful for correcting incorrect colour balance.
- **Colour effects** Some models allow you to produce sepia or black and white effects.

USEFUL PROCESSOR FEATURES

Some processors have more than one output, allowing you to make multiple copies. If your camcorder is hi-band, you need S-input.

Split screen is available on many processors, showing you the original image next to the enhanced image on the TV.

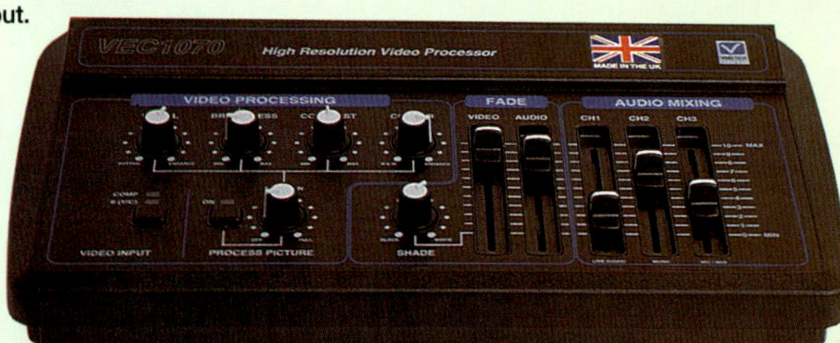

Audio controls are common on video processors. These may include manual volume to boost or reduce the sound level, or more than one input so that you can mix the original sound with music or commentary.

Enhancement features are the most commonly used controls on a processor. They allow you to alter the video signal to compensate for problems such as too much contrast or dark images.

Colour manipulation controls also appear on most video processors. These allow you to alter the overall colour or boost individual colours. They may also give you special effects such as sepia and black and white.

BLACK AND WHITE

By turning the colour intensity control right down, you can produce black and white images. Some people believe there is an atmospheric quality to black and white that is lacking in colour. It can be used to emulate a style or show a location that is colourless and uninteresting. You can combine its use with colour to contrast two different scenes or locations.

CONNECTION TO A PROCESSOR

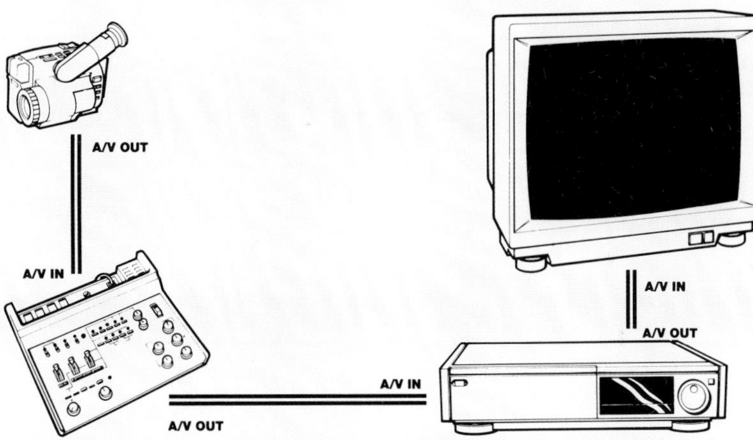

Processors fit between the camcorder and the VCR. Some processors have several video inputs and outputs. You can run the video output from the unit to several VCRs, making several copies of the tape.

If you need multiple copies, the normal route is to assemble edit one and make copies of it. The problem here is that the copies are poorer quality.

If you are passing the signal through other units, place the processor closest to the VCR.

FADES

A cut occurs when one shot ends and another begins immediately. The cut is not the only way of moving from one shot to another, however. The various methods are collectively known as transitions.

The second most common transition is the fade. A fade out occurs when the intensity of the shot is reduced until the image disappears. Normally, the screen fades to black, but it might fade to another colour.

A fade in occurs when the screen starts black and the intensity of the signal is increased until the image appears.

Fades can be produced in-camera or during editing. Many camcorders have fade buttons. When pressed, the camcorder reduces the size of the iris until it is closed. It also fades down the sound. Many editors and processors include fade controls for use during editing.

There are three types of fade, each with a traditional usage.

Fade out/cut in

This occurs when the first shot fades out and the second starts at full intensity. Fading out provides a slow cessation of action.

FADE OUT / CUT IN

Sometimes known as a punch intro, the fade out slows the pace of the action and the cut in delivers a slap in the face to the viewer. Use it to give impact to the second shot.

CUT OUT / FADE IN

The cut out/fade in slows down the pace of the action. It is useful when the first scene involves loud or fast action, but the second contains slower action and takes place some time later.

Fading out and cutting in jolts the viewer. It is suited to transitions where the first shot contains little movement or action, but where the second is dramatic. The longer the fade, the greater the jolt to the viewer when the next shot cuts in.

Fading out and cutting in can be used between shots in a montage sequence where you want each new subject to have impact. They can be too distracting in narrative scenes.

Cut out/fade in

This slows the pace of the action. It is normally reserved for transitions between scenes where the first scene contains loud or exciting action. The second takes place some time later and contains gentler action.

The intensity increases throughout the first scene then ends abruptly. A fade in gives the viewer time to adjust to the slower pace.

Fade out/fade in

The visual equivalent of the end of a chapter in a novel. It is most commonly used to indicate that time and action have moved on. A fade out/fade in can also be used to draw the viewer's attention to a significant action or subject.

An author might end a chapter at a point of high excitement or danger. The next chapter begins at exactly the same time and in the same location. The chapter end was used as a device to ensure the reader pauses to reflect on the significance of the action.

DISSOLVES

There are other transitions beyond cuts and fades. The most useful is the dissolve, or mix.

During a dissolve, one shot fades down, while the second fades up. Both shots appear on the screen together.

The differences between the cut and the dissolve have become blurred, but the cut is generally seen as a transition connecting two pieces of action occurring one straight after the other.

Dissolves often suggest the passing of time. They are useful for avoiding jump cuts, line crossing and errors in continuity of appearance.

Different times and places

If you cut between two shots of the same subject without changing shot size or angle, or if the subject's appearance changes between shots, you create a jump cut.

If you substitute a dissolve for the cut, the viewer accepts that time has passed, and no jump cut occurs. Dissolves are often used in this way to condense action.

When someone is performing an activity that takes several hours, you can show half a dozen shots of crucial points in the action. If you join the shots by cuts, there is a jump at every edit point. Dissolving between the shots smooths over the joins.

Dissolves can also join shots taking place in different locations, having the same value as the word 'meanwhile...'

Using dissolves

Dissolves can vary in length from a few frames to a few seconds. Long dissolves have a restful quality and are often used either to convey the passage of time or to join images in a montage sequence when you want a slow, restful pace.

Don't use dissolves constantly to avoid bad edits. The cut is designed to be invisible, whereas the dissolve is noticed by the viewer. Because of this, it tends to slow down the pace of the action, so constant use can destroy the build-up of tension or excitement.

Beyond dissolves are other transitions. The most common are wipes, where one picture wipes over another. These interrupt the flow of the video, so should be used sparingly.

A slow dissolve is often seen as an elegant way of moving from one shot to another. This transition might take several seconds. Don't use a slow dissolve in a scene containing action or movement. A half-second dissolve is better suited to fast action sequences where you want to show a short time has elapsed.

DISSOLVE SET-UP

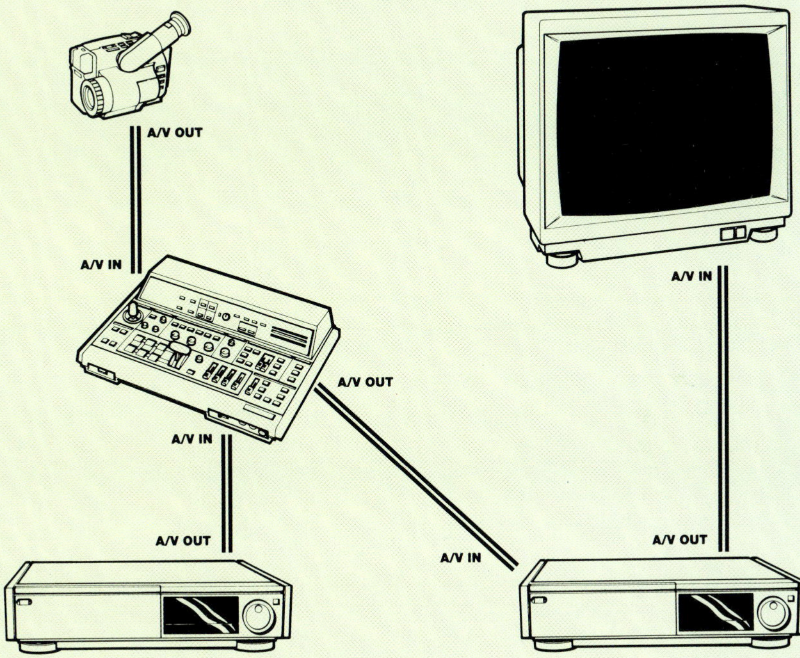

To dissolve between two shots you need a vision mixer with two video inputs. If both shots are on the same tape, you need to copy one shot to a second tape before you start. This gives two video sources, both connected to the vision mixer.

Connect the vision mixer to the record VCR. Copy the first shot, and release the pause on the second source just before you want the dissolve to start. Slide the mix lever from one input source to another. Pause the first source machine as soon as the image disappears.

TITLING

There are a number of ways of making your edited home movies look more professional. The most basic method is to add titles.

Many camcorders have a titling facility built in. This may be a caption generator or a digital superimposer.

Caption generators
These enable you to type in a small caption that can be superimposed over the video. The size and style of letters used is very limited and they usually offer one or two lines of text.

Because the camcorder has no keyboard built in, most captions have to be accessed by a menu system. This can be very time-consuming.

Digital superimposer
When you point the camcorder at a subject and press the digital superimpose store button, the camcorder takes a snapshot of the scene. It renders dark parts of the scene as black and light parts as white to produce a two-tone image.

If you press the store button while the camcorder is pointed at solid writing, the superimposer stores the caption. This means you can create titles in-camera using any type style or size you want.

With both caption generators and digital superimposers, you can normally select what colour you want the superimposed title to be.

TITLE SUPERIMPOSERS

Some camcorders allow you to create or store a title and superimpose it at the time of editing. This means you can select a title that is most suitable to the shot you want to superimpose it on.

If you are using the digital superimposer to record the caption, make sure the title you have created is fixed in one place and well lit. Rest the camcorder on a solid surface, such as a pile of books or a tripod, to ensure it is steady and at 90° to the title. Manually focus the lens.

When you superimpose the title at the editing stage, you can select the most appropriate position and lettering. Avoid the outside 10 per cent of the frame and choose a position where there is a solid mass of one colour.

Record a black title on white and change the colour in-camera. Light colours on dark stand out the most.

TITLE CARDS

If your camcorder has no titling facility, you can still create electronic titles by buying a dedicated unit. A handful of camcorders have sockets that allow you to plug in tiny caption generators for use at the time of shooting.

You will get better results by adding titles at the editing stage. You can buy a sophisticated titling unit or, alternatively, a number of edit controllers have titlers built in.

Title cards

If you want to be a little more creative, you can produce your own non-electronic titles. The simplest method is to draw or paint on a piece of card and record this as a separate shot to drop into your video at the appropriate point. This may be a project for someone with artistic flare.

Creative titles

Try one of the following:

- Arrange elements that are appropriate to the video on a table and include something with writing. Shoot from slightly above to see the three-dimensional effect.
- If you have a number of titles to add to the video, place them on a long sheet of paper and scroll them up. Mount the camcorder on a tripod.
- Place the individual titles on a flip chart and flip them over one by one.
- Simulate electronic titles by writing the titles on a sheet of glass or acetate and placing them in front of a photograph or painting.
- Place a title written on glass close to the lens and focus on a scene in the distance. The title will be virtually invisible. Pull focus from the background to the title.

For a really creative title, arrange a number of items that are relevant to the video on a table or on the floor. Don't place major elements right at the edge of the frame as they might distort. Place written material fairly prominently in the arrangement, and shoot from slightly above so you can see the full 3D effect.

ADDING TITLES

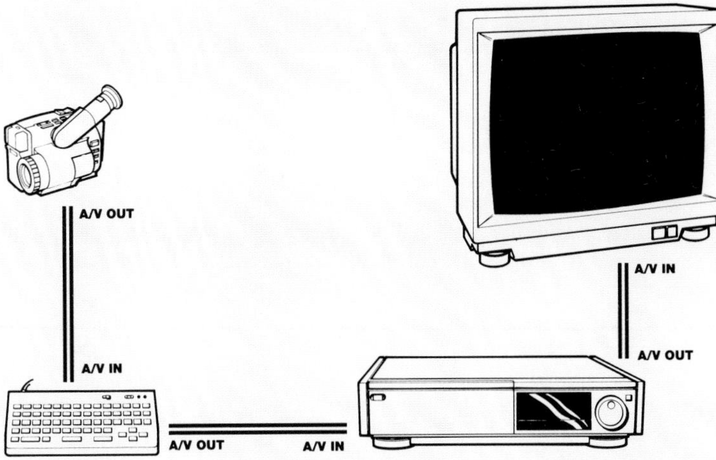

Buying an add-on titler gives you access to far more creative titles than you can produce in-camera. Apart from offering a variety of colours and type styles, many allow you to stretch letters, outline words and even make selected titles flash. They may even let you scroll words in from the side or the bottom of the frame.

The A/V leads from the camcorder feed through the titling unit to the VCR.

SUITABLE TYPEFACES

When creating your own titles, choose letters that are easy to read and not too small – a tenth of the screen height or larger.

Capital letters have greatest impact, so use them for short titles. A mixture of capital and lower-case letters is easier to read, so use them for longer titles.

Avoid fine typefaces, elaborate scripts and styles with thin outlines.

A Mixture of Upper- and Lower-Case Letters is Clear and Easy to Read

CAPITALS HAVE MORE IMPACT

A script face may be difficult to read unless it is very large

An outline face may break up on screen

COMPUTER VIDEO

Home computers are playing an increasing part in video post-production. With the right hardware and software packages, your computer can do the job of an edit controller, titling unit, vision mixer and special effects generator.

The four main systems are the Commodore Amiga, Atari, PC-compatibles and the Apple Macintosh. A colour monitor is essential.

Genlocks and digitizers

Some computers have a video output that lets you record the computer images directly on to your VCR. If yours does not, or if you want to overlay a computer-generated image on to a video signal, you need to feed both the computer and A/V signals through a genlock. When you create a title or graphic, the genlock makes the background invisible, so the title can be superimposed on the video signal.

More advanced are digitizers, which enable you to feed video images into the computer and manipulate them.

Chroma key system

This is the opposite of a genlock. With this system you can eliminate a colour from your video image. If the background is a solid block of this colour, you can superimpose the remaining video image over a computer-generated background.

COMPUTER SET-UP

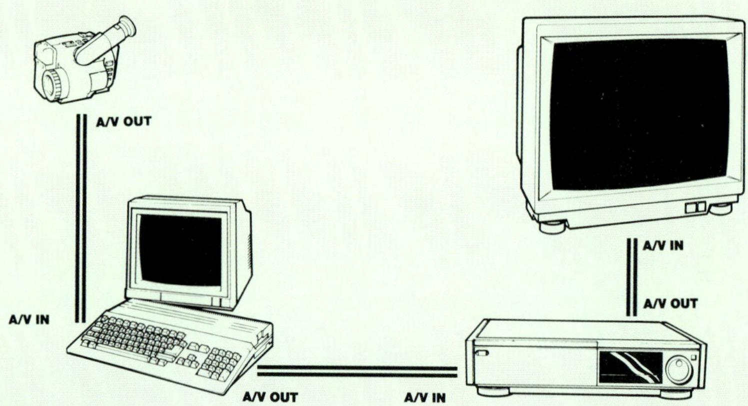

Genlocks come either as stand-alone units or as expansion cards to slot into the back of your computer. The video signal must pass through the genlock, into the computer, back out from the computer again and into the genlock. From here, the synchronized signal is sent to the VCR.

Some genlocks let you manipulate parts of the signal before recording.

TITLING

The most basic computer packages are for titling, although even the simplest are more sophisticated than most dedicated titling units.

Hundreds of colours can be selected, and there is a wide variety of type styles and sizes available. Systems generally let you scroll or fade titles into the video.

EDITING

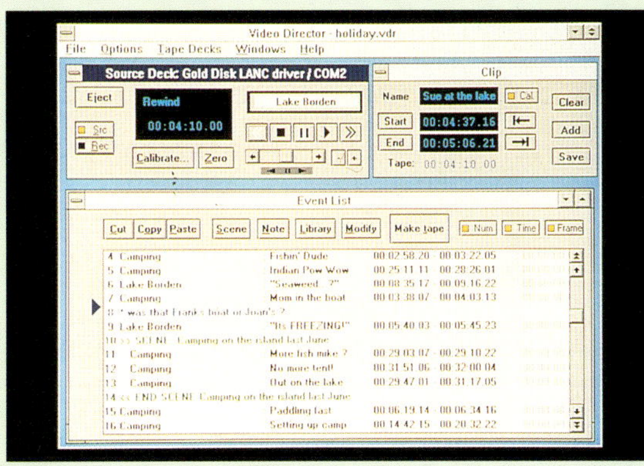

With a dedicated editing package you can perform all the functions available to you with a sophisticated edit controller. Some even offer time code facility.

Most software packages come with a hardware unit which controls the camcorder and VCR. The software controls the assemble editing process.

EFFECTS

If you get the right software, you can not only do away with a titler and editor, but also enhance the signal and manipulate it to change the image.

Some systems enable you to mix two video sources, so you can dissolve or wipe from one shot to another, or between video and computer images.

TIME LAPSE

For really creative scenes in a home movie, you can use time lapse or animation. With time lapse, you record a few frames at regular intervals. This enables you to condense a long time span into a very brief period of screen time.

A number of camcorders have time lapse built in. For camcorders with a Control-L socket, you can buy add-on interval timers that allow you to select the number of bursts of video you want to record, the duration of the shots and the interval between each shot.

Camcorders are not yet sophisticated enough to record one frame at a time, as they need to backspace over a few frames to ensure a clean edit. However, some can record a quarter to a half a second, which is usually good enough for time lapse.

Animation

Unfortunately, it is not accurate enough for proper animation, where lifeless objects or drawings appear to move. With animation you record a shot, move the subject slightly then record another shot. It is a time-consuming process, but you could provide endless amusement for children if you can animate their toys.

For animation to look professional, you need to record a shot every frame, but six- or seven- frame shots might be acceptable if you are shooting a home video for small children.

Although most camcorders don't have animation facilities, experiment yourself by pressing the record button very briefly, then pausing. Even if you don't get true animation, you will get an interesting effect.

Using time lapse over a long period can produce bizarre scenes, such as this model being built in under a minute. You can only record such scenes, however, if you can keep the camcorder and tripod set up in the same place for the duration.

As the sun travels across the sky, the light and reflections in a scene change drastically during the day. However, as this process takes several hours, the changes are hard to perceive – unless there is some instantaneous change, such as when the

COMPUTER ANIMATION

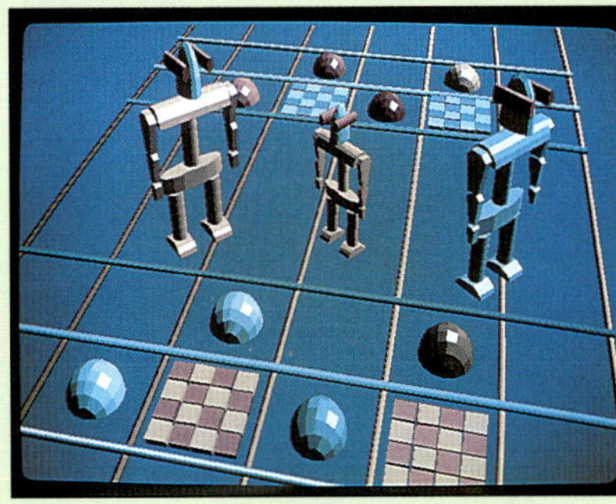

For professional-looking animation, you need to record a shot every frame, although every two frames is acceptable. Any longer and the movements appear extremely jerky.

The only way to produce really impressive animation with video is to use a sophisticated computer software package. With a genlock you can combine live video with animation.

Software packages vary greatly in price and sophistication, but some allow you to animate cartoon animals and people so they appear to walk.

Learning to program animation sequences is often a time-consuming process, but the results can be very impressive.

sun passes briefly behind a cloud.

With time lapse you can condense this process into a fraction of the time, maybe only 20 or 30 seconds. Stand the camcorder on a tripod and time it so that you record a few frames every 10 minutes or so.

Time lapse can be used for dramatic effect, showing how people crowd into a location at certain times during the day, or for educational documentaries, showing such subjects as flowers opening or a bird building a nest.

DOCUMENTARIES

"When you get more advanced, you may be called on to make a documentary video.

"My documentary was about my local flying club, and it followed the progress of a new member until his first solo flight.

"Hobbies always make good subjects for documentaries, but you might also want to make a profile of a person or place, or even a campaigning video."

"No documentary is complete without at least one interview. It is important that the scene is shot and edited so that we appear to be looking at each other." (See *Sight Lines*, p. 82.)

"Camcorders have white balance systems to ensure that the colours in a scene are rendered accurately." (See *White Balance*, p. 52.)

"When people are walking, it can be difficult to follow them and keep the camcorder steady. A useful device designed for recording on the move is the Steadicam JR."
(See *Steadicam JR*, p. 15.)

"The climax of my documentary was the first solo flight. I was in a plane for this shot, so that I could look down on the glider." (See *Looking Down*, p. 25.)

"This cutaway helps to condense time, so that I could miss out some of the flight without it looking as if any of the action scenes of the glider had been cut." (See *Cutaways*, p. 86.)

"Whenever you show a person looking or pointing, the viewer assumes the next shot is what they are looking at. This helps them build up a picture of the location in their mind."
(See *Spatial Connections*, p. 88.)

5

Sound

Sound Systems
Basic Sound
Add-on Microphones
Audio Dubbing
Sound Mixing

SOUND SYSTEMS

Sound is as important to home movies as picture quality. Yet many videos are ruined by appalling soundtracks. A shot may show a conversation, but the soundtrack contains nothing but traffic noise.

The brain is very good at filtering out distracting noise and discerning particular sounds. Camcorders, however, record sounds as the microphone 'hears' them. Whereas a person can ignore an aeroplane flying overhead, the noise is faithfully reproduced by the camcorder.

Recording methods

Although camcorders record sound in the same general way, they use a variety of systems.

- **VHS** This uses two systems, linear mono and hi-fi stereo. With linear mono, the sound is recorded on a narrow track on the edge of the tape. With hi-fi stereo the sound is recorded on two tracks (left and right), which are stored on the same portion of the tape as the picture signal. Having more room to store the signal means they can more faithfully reproduce the sound. VHS hi-fi stereo camcorders also have a linear mono track.
- **8mm** These camcorders use a soundtrack that is also recorded with the picture signal. Better models have two soundtracks for stereo recording.

The most advanced 8mm system is PCM stereo. This is a digital track with its own area on the tape.

WHERE SOUND IS RECORDED

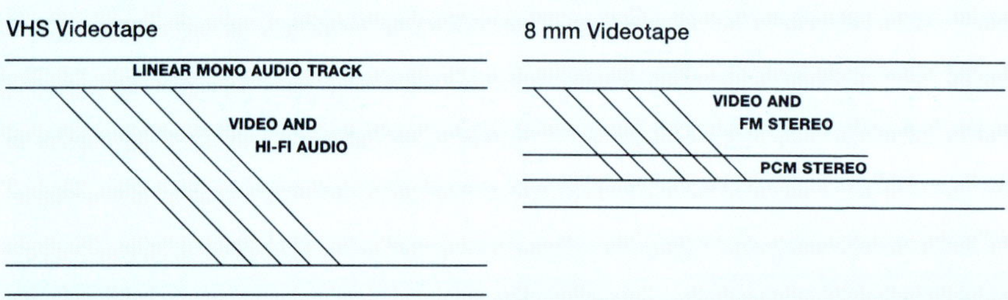

Sound is recorded in a different place on the tape according to the format. Information is written and read by tiny recording and playback 'heads' mounted on a spinning cylinder called a head drum.

The head drum spins very rapidly and diagonally to the tape direction. The picture information is thus recorded diagonally. VHS hi-fi stereo and 8mm mono and hi-fi stereo sound are also laid down diagonally on the tape, using heads situated on the head drum.

Linear mono is recorded on the edge of the VHS tape by a stationary recording head. Less tape per second runs past this head than past spinning heads, so less information is recorded.

PCM tracks are recorded by heads on the revolving head drum, but are stored on a different portion of the tape from the video signal.

SYSTEM	DESCRIPTION	PROS	CONS
LINEAR MONO	The standard system for budget VHS and VHS-C camcorders	Recorded on a separate part of the tape from the video signal, so each can be rerecorded independently. Found on cheaper camcorders	Poorer quality than hi-fi systems
8mm MONO	The sound recording system found on cheaper 8mm camcorders	Capable of storing more information than linear mono, leading to better sound quality. Camcorders with 8mm mono tend to be inexpensive	Recorded in the same place on the tape as the picture, so one cannot be recorded separately from the other
8mm HI-FI STEREO	Found on Hi8 camcorders and on some better 8mm camcorders	Records on two separate tracks - left and right - and gives more realistic sound recording than mono systems	Sound and picture recorded in the same place on the tape, so cannot be recorded separately. Camcorders often more expensive than mono versions
VHS HI-FI STEREO	Found on S-VHS-C, S-VHS and some VHS and VHS-C camcorders	Better quality than mono. Stereo VHS camcorders also have a linear mono track, so you can record new sound but keep existing sound on the hi-fi tracks	Tends to be found on more expensive camcorders. Any sound added to linear tracks is poorer quality than sound on hi-fi tracks
PCM STEREO	Found only on top-end Hi8 models	Exceptionally high quality. Recorded in separate place from picture, so can be rerecorded without affecting video signal. PCM models also have hi-fi stereo	Camcorders with PCM tend to be expensive

BASIC SOUND

How close you should stand to your subject for good sound recording depends on a number of factors, including how loud it is and what type of environment you are recording in.

With practice, you become aware of the limitations of your camcorder's sound recording system. To get a basic idea, ask a friend to stand a few feet away from the camcorder and start talking. Record about ten seconds or so, then ask her to stand further away and record her again. Repeat this for a number of different distances and environments, both indoor and out.

You may be surprised at how close a person has to stand to be heard clearly in a noisy environment.

Auto gain control

Camcorders don't record sound at a constant level. In quiet environments, the recording volume is increased. This facility is called AGC (auto gain control).

Outside, when there may be a lot of background noise, the AGC is set at a low level, so the speaker has to stand close to be heard. Inside, if they are standing away from the camcorder, the AGC is boosted, so their speech can be recorded clearly.

When the AGC is boosted, quiet sounds, such as the operating noise of the camcorder's autofocus or zoom motors, may be recorded. The answer again is to stand close to your subject.

ACOUSTICS

When recording inside, the sound you record comes mainly from its source. Unwanted sound may also come from sound waves reflected off walls or furnishings. Metal and glass are extremely reflective, wood and plastic slightly less so. Soft fabrics, curtains and cushions absorb sound.

Absorbent environments give a more even sound, whereas reflective environments can cause echoes and distortions in the form of a hollow boom.

You can increase the absorbency of a room by placing cushions and drapes against reflective surfaces off-camera.

WIND NOISE

When you are outside, you have very little control over background noise. Listen out for any interfering sounds. Get your subjects to stand close to you, speaking slowly and clearly. Any mumbling will be lost outdoors.

A major problem outdoors is wind noise. Try to shield the camcorder from the wind. Sheets of card, reflectors and umbrellas make ideal wind breaks.

MONITORING

As the human hearing system filters out distracting noise, the only way to be sure what the camcorder is recording is to monitor the sound through a set of headphones.

When you monitor sound in this way, you can quickly determine if there is interference from other sound. Some camcorders also let you control the recording level manually.

ADD-ON MICROPHONES

If your movies are persistently dogged by poor sound, it may be due to the limitations of your equipment. The weakest link in the chain is the microphone (mic).

Many camcorders have microphone inputs for accessory mics. If you are some distance from your subject, ask an assistant to hold the add-on mic close to the subject. Ideally, the mic should be positioned on the end of a wooden pole, known as a boom.

Field of coverage

The most important distinction between different microphones is field of coverage, or pick-up pattern. This describes how sensitive the mic is to sounds from different directions.

There are four types of mic designed for use with camcorders.

- **Omnidirectional mics** have a 360° field of coverage, which means they are equally sensitive to sounds coming from all directions. They are particularly useful for picking up general atmospheric noise in a scene.
- **Cardioid mics**, which are generally fitted to camcorders, are far more sensitive to sound coming from the front than sounds from the rear. If a person needs to stand 2 metres from you to be heard with an omnidirectional mic, they will still be heard at around 3.5 metres with a cardioid.
- **Supercardioids** have a narrower field of coverage – about 120° in front of the mic. This makes them particularly useful for more distant subjects. If 2 metres is the limit for an omnidirectional mic, a supercardioid will still pick up what is being said up to 8 metres away.
- **Hypercardioid mics** have a pick-up pattern of 90° or narrower. They can successfully record a sound at 12 metres that the omnidirectional could only record up to 2 metres. Very loud sounds coming from any direction are always recorded, whatever the mic.

OMNIDIRECTIONAL

Use an omnidirectional microphone to record general atmospheric sound from all around, such as here at a street market, or for crowd noise at a sports match.

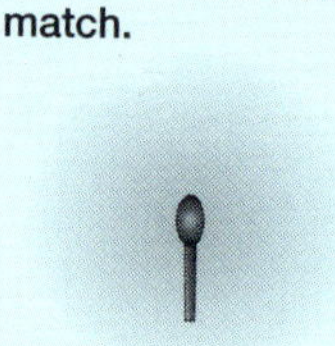

CARDIOID

A good all-round mic, the cardioid is useful for picking up conversations and sound from directly in front of the it. Turned upright and held low the cardioid can also double as an omni-directional mic.

SUPERCARDIOID

With a supercardioid mic you can stand further from your subject than with a cardioid, and still hear the sound clearly. The optimum distance depends on the level of background noise.

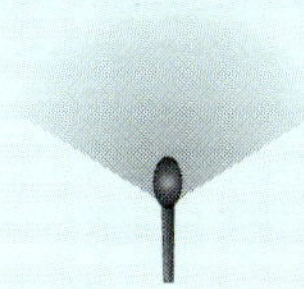

HYPERCARDIOID

A hypercardioid mic is useful when you can't stand close to the subject, but recording the sound in detail is important. Aiming the mic becomes more important with a hypercardioid.

EQUIPMENT CARE

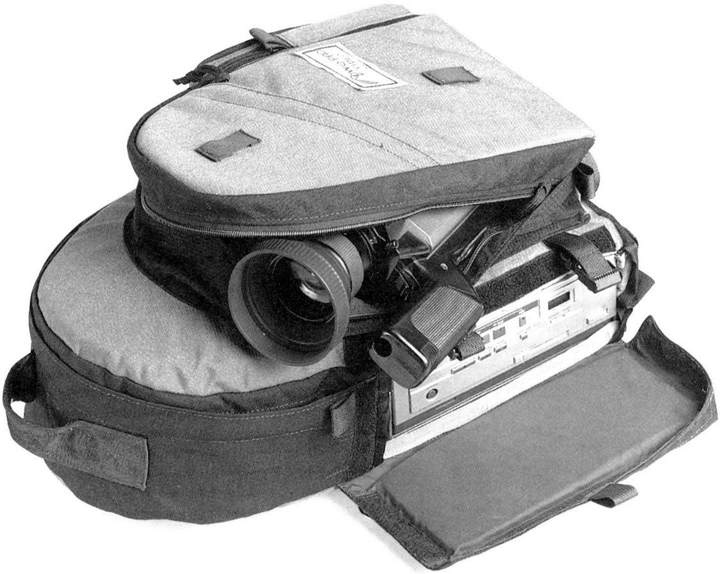

Camcorder Care

Camcorders are the most sophisticated pieces of equipment most people own. Although they are well built, they are expensive and contain delicate electronics, so you have to handle them with care.

Tips for care

• Make sure the camcorder is not subjected to rain or damp. Waterproof protective housings are available if you are shooting in wet conditions.

• Sudden changes in temperature can cause condensation to appear on the video heads and on the lens elements. If you are moving from cold outdoors to warm indoors, leave the camcorder to acclimatize before storing it away.

• Don't leave the camcorder exposed in bright sunlight. Some of the circuits within the camcorder are sensitive to temperature. In extreme heat, the current flowing through them can be increased, blowing some fuses. The camcorder will then have to be serviced before you can use it again.

• It is also important that the camcorder is not placed for any time under bright studio lights. The camcorder's plastic housing may warp in intense heat, and lubricating grease used to help the lens elements move smoothly can melt.

• Radio or TV transmitters can disrupt your picture, so don't video in their immediate proximity.

ADDING A WILDTRACK

SOUND	AMBIENT SOUND WILDTRACK

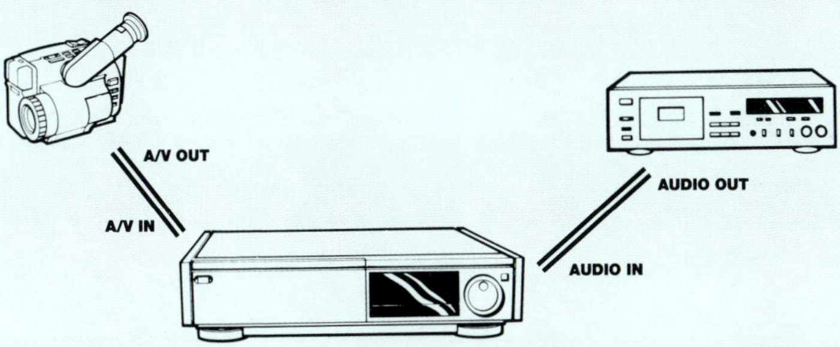

Instead of music, you can add a wildtrack. This is a continuous recording of background sound that either replaces the original sound or is mixed in with it. Here, the general hum of the carnival provides the wildtrack. The video sequence is recorded first and the wildtrack audio dubbed later.

ASSEMBLE EDITED SEQUENCE
AUDIO DUBBED GREEK FOLK MUSIC

SOUND MIXING

In most home movies, the soundtrack consists of sound recorded at the time of shooting (known as the sync sound). In professional productions, a lot more is added at the editing stage.

Sound mixers

Adding sound during post-production is called sweetening. You can sweeten your home videos easily with an inexpensive sound mixer.

Sound mixers have a number of audio inputs and one output. Into the inputs go different sound sources, such as microphones, CD players and your camcorder's audio out. Each source has a volume control so you can set the correct level for each.

Sound effects and commentary can be added while assemble editing. Music and wildtracks are continuous and so can only be audio dubbed on to an already assembled video.

Adding music and wildtracks

If you want to mix music or a wildtrack on to an edited sequence without losing the sync sound, you have three choices:

- Record the music and/or wildtrack on to the video recorder first. Use the VCR's insert edit facility to add the video and sync sound.
- Assemble edit the video, then audio dub the music or wildtrack on to the tape. To add both music and wildtrack, you need a sound mixer.
- Assemble edit the shots then copy the assembled video sequence on to a second VCR (see diagram). While copying, mix the sync sound from the first VCR with the output from a tape or CD player, using a sound mixer. Run the audio out from the mixer to the second VCR's audio input.

The disadvantage of the last method is that you have to copy twice, reducing picture quality.

- Sync sound is recorded at the time of shooting. For the first and last shots, we used a hypercardioid mic to record the sounds of physical exertion. For the second shot, we used a cardioid mic.
- Sound effects of a ball being kicked were recorded afterwards with the mic next to the ball. These were added at the right moments and sounded far more convincing than the live sound, which was lost in the general noise of the match.
- A wildtrack of crowd and traffic noise was recorded at the event and added to the sequence.
- You can add music at dramatic moments or commentary to make a documentary.

SYNC SOUND	EXERTION
SFX	—
WILDTRACK	CROWD NOISE

USING A SOUND MIXER

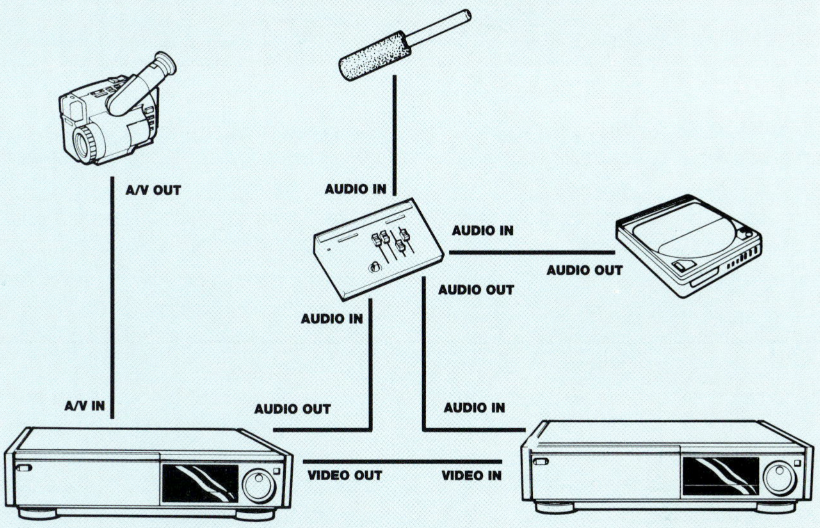

If you have a hi-fi VCR with insert edit or audio dub, you can copy the video and the mixed audio signals separately. If not, you can still add extra sound to your home movie with a sound mixer.

First, assemble edit your video on to VCR1. If you have edited your shots in-camera, you don't need to assemble edit on a VCR, and can use your camcorder instead of VCR1.

Next, connect the video signal from VCR1 to VCR2. Run the audio output lead carrying the sync sound to one of the inputs of a sound mixer. Mix it with other sound sources while copying to VCR 2.

SHOUTING
—
CONTINUOUS CROWD NOISE

EXERTION
BALL BEING KICKED
CONTINUOUS CROWD NOISE

EQUIPMENT CARE

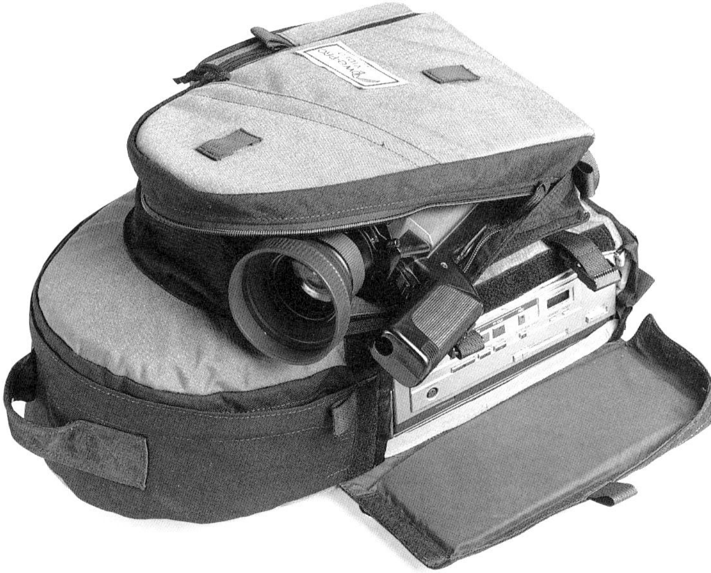

Camcorder Care

Camcorders are the most sophisticated pieces of equipment most people own. Although they are well built, they are expensive and contain delicate electronics, so you have to handle them with care.

Tips for care

• Make sure the camcorder is not subjected to rain or damp. Waterproof protective housings are available if you are shooting in wet conditions.

• Sudden changes in temperature can cause condensation to appear on the video heads and on the lens elements. If you are moving from cold outdoors to warm indoors, leave the camcorder to acclimatize before storing it away.

• Don't leave the camcorder exposed in bright sunlight. Some of the circuits within the camcorder are sensitive to temperature. In extreme heat, the current flowing through them can be increased, blowing some fuses. The camcorder will then have to be serviced before you can use it again.

• It is also important that the camcorder is not placed for any time under bright studio lights. The camcorder's plastic housing may warp in intense heat, and lubricating grease used to help the lens elements move smoothly can melt.

• Radio or TV transmitters can disrupt your picture, so don't video in their immediate proximity.

Lens Care

All camcorders have zoom lenses built in. The majority offer 6x or 8x magnification, but longer ranges are available. Video systems can resolve much less information than photographic film; the quality demands on camcorder lenses are therefore much lower than the demands on still camera lenses, so all camcorder lenses give acceptable quality.

Tips for care

Although the internal lens elements are protected by the camcorder shell, the front of the lens can be easily damaged if not treated with care.

- Protect the lens by keeping the lens cap on at all times except when you are shooting.
- When the camcorder is in use, screw a protective or UV filter on to the front of the lens. This will have little effect on the image, but it will stop the front element of the lens from being scratched or damaged.
- If you get smudges on the lens, don't use an abrasive cloth. Special lens-cleaning cloths are available from photo specialists.

Focal length

Focal lengths give a rough idea of the angle of view that the lens can see. The smaller the focal length, the wider the angle of view. A typical wide-angle setting on a zoom lens might be 9 mm, with the focal length at the telephoto setting around 54 mm.

A 9 mm focal length on one camcorder does not necessarily give the same angle of view as a 9 mm lens setting on another. The diameter of the imaging chip is also a factor. Most camcorders contain a ⅓ in CCD imaging chip, with some larger models using a ½ in CCD. A small number contain a ⅔ in.

Many people are familiar with the focal lengths of 35 mm still camera lenses, which are the same for all 35 mm compacts and SLRs. The following table gives an approximate guide to the angle of view at various focal lengths.

	Angle of view	⅓ in CD	½ in CCD	⅔ in CCD	35 mm SLR equivalent
with 0.4x wide converter	115°	2.3 mm	3.4 mm	4.4 mm	20 mm
with 0.6x wide converter	76.6°	3.4 mm	5.1 mm	6.7 mm	30 mm
Typical wide-angle	46°	5.7 mm	8.6 mm	11 mm	50 mm
6x telephoto	7.6°	34.5 mm	51.7 mm	66 mm	300 mm
8x telephoto	5.7°	46 mm	68.9 mm	88 mm	400 mm
12x telephoto	3.8°	69 mm	103.4 mm	132 mm	600 mm
64x digital zoom	0.7°	368 mm	551.7 mm	710 mm	3200 mm
12x converter on 6x zoom	0.6°	415 mm	620.6 mm	800 mm	3600 mm

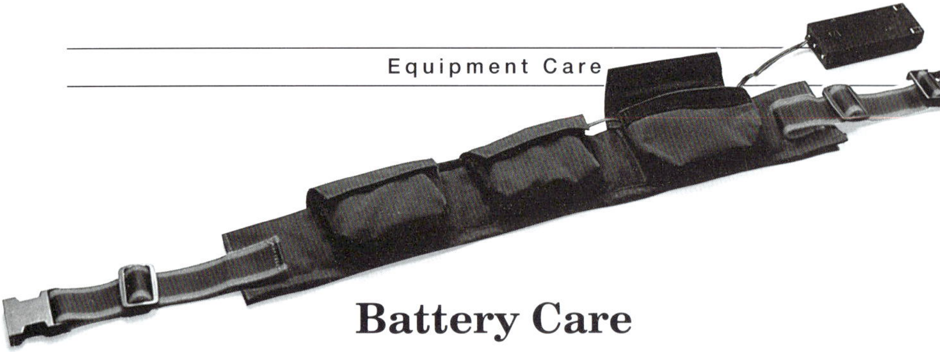

Battery Care

Camcorders can run off the mains, via a car adaptor or directly from a battery. Most camcorders use NiCad (Nickel Cadmium) batteries. A second battery is one of the most useful investments you can make. There are several models on the market, so check before you buy that it is the correct fit.

For emergencies, or if you are away from power supplies, you can buy an extra battery pack (EBP). This is a battery-shaped hollow pack that can take standard alkaline batteries.

Tips for battery care

- Most batteries give around an hour's shooting. Some functions use battery power more than others, but the tape transport controls are the biggest offenders. Constantly reviewing what you have shot consumes a lot of battery power.
- Fully discharge the battery before you use it again. If you frequently recharge the battery while it still has power in it, you may permanently lower the battery's power. Many chargers discharge the battery first.
- Make sure the battery is fully charged before you begin to use it. Otherwise, you have no way of knowing how much running time the battery will give you.
- Battery chemicals are sensitive to extremes of temperature. Recharge batteries at room temperature. Too cold, and charging takes longer. Too warm, and the batteries might not charge fully.
- Don't leave the battery on the camcorder when not in use as it will discharge slowly. Store it in a cool environment, lying flat.
- If the two contacts on your battery are connected by a conductive material, your battery can be short-circuited and ruined. Keep it in its protective plastic case when not attached to the camcorder.

Left: All camcorders are supplied with battery chargers, although other brands are available.

Top: If you shoot outside, you may find a battery belt a useful investment. Some versions give several hours' recording time.

Tape Care

With video tape, many people simply look at the price tag before they buy. But a good quality video tape can make a difference to the sound and picture quality of a home movie.

Tape is coated with tiny particles which are magnetized to store the audio and video signals. The smaller these particles, and the tighter they are packed, the more information they can store.

Tape grades

Different manufacturers use different methods of coating video tape. They also rate them according to their performance, giving them names such as high grade, super high grade, extra high grade and pro. The problem is that so long as tapes pass a basic standard, they can be called anything the manufacturer wants.

Well-known brands tend to be more scrupulous about producing better quality video tape than some cheaper suppliers, so the general rule is to stick with the major brands and opt for professional (pro) grade tape. The camcorder tape market suffers less from cheap, low-quality products than the standard VHS market.

Keep tapes away from strong magnetic sources. However, airport X-ray machines won't damage or erase your recordings. Avoid heat, damp and intense sunlight.

Stick to good quality tapes from well-known brands. Cheap tapes are more likely to shed parts of their magnetic coating, clogging up your camcorder or VCR's record and playback heads.

Lamp Care

In video, not only is the quantity of light important, but the quality too. Add-on lights help you control both. Powerful lamps are useful accessories for indoors, but they are delicate and should be handled with care.

Tips for care

• The bulbs become more fragile when lit, so avoid moving or knocking them. Wait for them to cool for ten minutes before moving to a new location or packing away.

• Avoid handling the bulbs, even when cold. Use a cloth, as some bulbs can be damaged by skin moisture.

• Don't place anything too close to the bulb when in use. It gets very hot and some materials will burn or melt. Use proper holders for flags or cookies.

• Avoid using lamps in damp areas or where there is a danger of them being splashed by water.

• Use insulation tape to secure cables and leads to the floor to prevent anyone tripping over them or unbalancing the lamp. Make sure the lamp is stable on its stand.

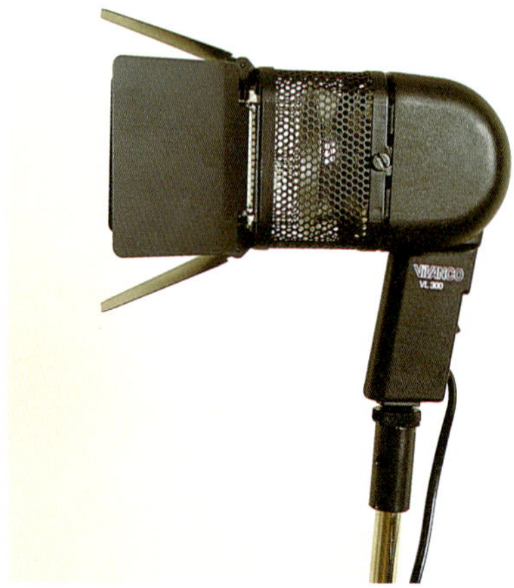

Treat all video lamps with care. Don't handle them roughly when they are hot, and tape down any trailing power leads.

• Don't leave lamps on when not in use. They drain a lot of power and can become very hot.

• If you are using a number of lights, ask an electrician to look over your electrics and advise you on safety.

• Be careful with lights when there are children or animals around.

Accessory Care

All video accessories can come in useful at some time, but you are unlikely to need all of them on every video excursion. If you are travelling about by car, you can take what you like with you. But if carriage is a problem, you have to be very selective.

Bags are essential for people who want to carry a number of accessories with them. Soft bags are light and easy to carry, but hard bags offer greater protection. Some bags have movable compartments, so you can customize them for your accessories.

Supports

Supports are useful, as handheld shots can look a bit shaky. If you always carry a tripod around with you, it saves you hunting around for walls and natural supports.

Filters

Filters can alter the recorded image in many ways. Not all camcorders are fitted with the same diameter thread; check your instruction manual.

Some camcorders feature an auto-focus system known as inner focusing (these are the models without a manual zoom lever). With inner focusing, the front element of the lens (including the filter thread) rotates when the camcorder refocuses.

Some filters (e.g. polarizing filters) have a different effect depending on their orientation. When using one of these, focus, then rotate the filter.

Accessories are available to help you improve all areas of your movie-making.

The most useful accessories are a spare battery and some form of support.

Format Compatibility

There are six camcorder formats, which are divided into the VHS and the 8mm families.

The four VHS formats (VHS, VHS-C, S-VHS and S-VHS-C) all use tape that has a ½-inch diameter. The 'S' stands for super, and signifies denser, smaller particles on the tape and a more sophisticated signal processing system in the hardware. The 'C' stands for compact, and refers to the size of cassette the tape is housed in.

There are two formats in the 8mm family, standard 8mm and Hi8. Hi8 is the equivalent to S-VHS and S-VHS-C, and the three are collectively known as hi-band formats. As the names suggest, both 8mm and Hi8 use tape with an 8mm diameter.

Compatibility

Compatibility between the two families is non-existent. Within the families, compatibility is partial. Although full-sized cassettes won't fit in compact camcorders, C-format tapes may play in VHS VCRs when housed in an adaptor. The tables below show the compatibility between cassettes, camcorders and VCRs.

8mm FAMILY	Camcorder/VCR	
Cassette	8mm	Hi8
blank 8mm	records OK	records OK, 8mm quality
blank Hi8	records OK, 8mm quality	records OK
recorded 8mm	plays OK	plays OK, 8mm quality
recorded Hi8	won't play	plays OK, Hi8 quality

VHS FAMILY	Camcorder/VCR			
Cassette	VHS	S-VHS	VHS-C	S-VHS-C
blank VHS	records OK	records OK VHS quality	won't fit	won't fit
blank S-VHS	records OK VHS quality	records OK	won't fit	won't fit
blank VHS-C	records with adaptor	records with adaptor VHS quality	records OK	records OK, VHS quality
blank S-VHS-C	records with adaptor VHS quality	records with adaptor	records OK, VHS quality	records OK
recorded VHS	plays OK	plays OK, VHS quality	won't fit	won't fit
recorded S-VHS	won't play	plays OK	won't fit	won't fit
recorded VHS-C	OK with adaptor	OK with adaptor, VHS quality	plays OK	plays OK, VHS quality
recorded S-VHS-C	won't play	OK with adaptor	won't play	plays OK

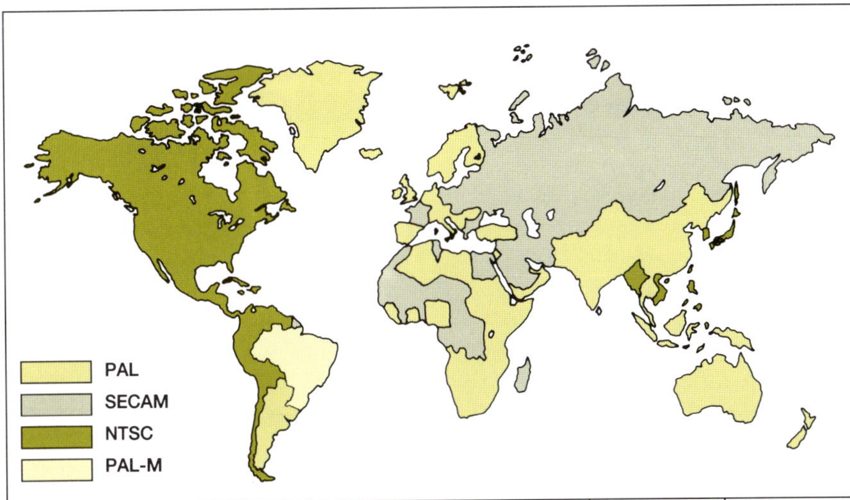

		PAL	SECAM	NTSC	PAL-M
Chrominance		PAL	SECAM	NTSC	PAL
Luminance	Scanning lines	625 lines	625 lines	525 lines	525 lines
	Field frequency	50Hz	50Hz	60Hz	60Hz

Standards Compatibility

Pre-recorded video cassettes bought in one part of the world may be incompatible with VCRs elsewhere if the two countries have different TV standards. Blank tapes are the same wherever you buy them.

There are three basic standards: PAL, NTSC and SECAM. Broadly, PAL is used in Europe, Africa, China, Australia and India; NTSC in Japan, the USA and Canada; SECAM in France, Central Africa, the Middle East and Russia. A few countries have adopted hybrid systems, such as the PAL-M (525 lines, 60Hz) system used in Brazil.

PAL and SECAM both contain 625 horizontal lines, and both use a scanning rate of 50 fields per second (expressed as 50Hz – see p. 50). Pre-recorded tapes in one standard play back in black and white in the other.

NTSC contains 525 horizontal lines and scans at a rate of 60Hz. This means it is completely incompatible with the other two systems.

TAPE STANDARD	**VIDEO RECORDER STANDARD**			
	PAL 625/50	**SECAM 625/50**	**NTSC 525/60**	**PAL-M 525/60**
PAL 625/50	plays OK	b/w only	won't play	won't play
SECAM 625/50	b/w only	plays OK	won't play	won't play
NTSC 525/60	won't play	won't play	plays OK	b/w only
PAL-M 525/60	won't play	won't play	b/w only	plays OK

Glossary

Acoustics Sound characteristics of an environment. Hard surfaces tend to increase the amount of echo recorded.

Aspect ratio Relative dimensions of the film or video image, governed by the dimensions of the screen on which it is to be viewed. Camcorders, like conventional TVs, have aspect ratios of 4:3 – four parts wide to three parts down. Widescreen TVs have aspect ratios of 16:9; most cinema screens are wider.

Assemble edit Method of editing that involves copying shots one by one from one tape to another.

Audio dub All VHS formats have a mono audio track at the edge of the tape that can be recorded independently from the picture and any hi-fi stereo sound. Audio dub is the feature on a camcorder or VCR that allows this track to be recorded without the picture being affected.

Audio jump cuts Jumps in background sound occurring at the edit point when the camcorder is paused briefly. Most noticeable with background music.

A/V (audio/video) splitter Any device capable of taking an incoming video and/or audio signal and outputting more than one identical signal. Some processors also act as A/V splitters.

Back light Light placed behind the subject to produce an attractive halo and pick out the shape of the subject. Light from the back light should not shine directly into the lens.

Backlight compensation (BLC) Camcorder button causing either the iris to open or the video gain to be amplified so that a brighter signal is recorded, correctly exposing a dark foreground subject.

Backspacing Feature found on all camcorders and most VCRs that ensures edit points are free from interference. However, because it rewinds the tape slightly to do so, it affects the accuracy of the edit point.

Boom Long pole to which an off-camera microphone is secured, allowing it to be placed above or below subject, out of shot, but close enough to pick up sounds clearly.

Bounced light Hard light bounced off a white surface to turn it into a softer, more diffuse light.

Buffer shot Shot taken from on the line of action that has the effect of temporarily cancelling the line. From a buffer shot, you can record from either side of the line without confusing the viewer.

Camera shake Wobbly image caused by the camcorder not being held firmly. Because the image is magnified, camera shake is more extreme at the telephoto lens setting.

Caption generator Method of creating titles and captions in-camera. Titles are typed using either an accessory keyboard or via a menu system displayed in the viewfinder.

CCD (charge-coupled device) Silicon chip within the camcorder that, like film in a still camera, records the images passing through the lens and transfers them electronically to tape.

Chroma key Computer-based system that works by removing one colour from a scene. For example, if the background is this colour, the foreground subject can be superimposed on a different background.

Continuity errors Errors resulting from recording shots either out of sequence or with large time periods in between. Appearance of subject changes between shots.

Cookie Patterned screen, either bought or home-made, that can be placed in front of a light beam for a creative effect.

Cutaway Shot inserted into a sequence showing scenes close to or related to the main action. Can either be active (time-based), such as a clock face or people clapping, or passive (not time-based), such as spectators.

Day for night Technique for making daylight scenes look like moonlit scenes. Achieved by underexposing and using a blue filter.

Depth of field The amount of the scene in front of and behind the point being focused on that is also sharp. Increase depth of field by increasing subject distance, reducing size of iris and using wider lens settings.

Diffuser Any substance placed in front of a hard light source to scatter light and turn it into a soft light.

Digital superimposer Method of producing titles in-camera by pointing the lens at lettering and storing the image in a memory. The background is rendered transparent so the title can be superimposed on live video.

Digitizer Unit that allows video images to be manipulated by a computer.

Dissolve When two shots overlap, so that the first fades down on screen as the second fades up.

Dutch Tilt Effect produced when the camcorder is twisted to the side, so that the horizon appears diagonal in the frame.

Edit controller Device for controlling the functions of a camcorder and VCR or two VCRs. Many can be programmed to assemble edit shots automatically.

Edit point The join between one shot and another.

Establishing shot Shot at the start of a scene that lets the viewer know where the scene takes place.

Exposure The amount of light registered by the CCD. Exposure can be increased by opening the iris or boosting the gain to make the CCD more sensitive.

Field An individual image recorded by the camcorder. Technically only a half-image, as only half of the lines on the CCD record at any one time.

Field of coverage The sensitivity of a microphone to sounds coming from different directions. Mics with a narrow field of coverage are more sensitive to sounds coming from the front than the rear. Omnidirectional mics are equally sensitive to sounds from all directions.

Fill light Soft, low-powered light used to lift shadows on a subject and lower the contrast between light and dark areas.

Flags Any solid object placed in front of a light beam to stop light falling on a particular part of the image.

Flying erase head Recording head on a camcorder or VCR's head drum that operates during backspacing to ensure a clean edit point.

Frame Two consecutive fields (one odd line, one even) interlaced to form a complete video still.

Gain Amplification of the current being fed to the CCD to enable it to register an image. Boosting the gain increases the exposure. Audio gain increases recording volume in quiet environments.

Genlock Unit for synchronizing two signals (either video or computer generated), so they can be mixed.

Head drum Rapidly-spinning cylinder inside a camcorder or VCR's transport mechanism that contains a number of recording and playback 'heads'. These 'write' audio and video information on the tape during recording and 'read' the information during playback.

Hi-band Collective name for the S-VHS, S-VHS-C and Hi8 formats. The colour (chrominance) and brightness (luminance) parts of the video signal are processed separately to minimize interference.

Hosepiping Uncoordinated panning as a result of poor technique.

Hot spots Reflective areas of an image rendered overbright by strong lighting.

Image stabilization Systems built into camcorders to limit camera shake when hand-holding. There are two methods, electronic and optical. The former causes a slight drop in image quality, but is cheaper.

In-camera editing Most basic method of editing that relies on making all editing decisions at the time of shooting, so that when you record the final shot on the tape, the video is finished.

Indecisive cut Cutting between two shots of the same subject, but changing the shot size only slightly, so that the subject appears to jump in the frame.

Insert editing Method of editing that involves copying sound and pictures on to a tape, then copying new picture (or sound and picture) over portions of the video, but leaving the sound of the original shot intact.

Iris Variable-sized opening between the lens and CCD which can open and close to increase or reduce the exposure. The wider the iris used, the narrower the depth of field.

Jog/shuttle Two independently controlled dials on a VCR used to move the tape forward or backward at various speeds. Makes locating the correct position on the tape easier.

Jump cut A bad cut that jolts the viewer, normally because of the similarity of composition between the two shots. Best avoided by changing shot size and angle when shooting two shots of the same subject.

Key light The primary source of illumination on a subject. Usually a hard light.

Line of action Imaginary line drawn between two people in a scene or along the path of a moving subject to help organize camera positions. By crossing the line and shooting from the opposite side, you change a subject's screen direction, so a subject moving in one direction will appear to turn round.

Lux level The intensity of light in a scene. All camcorders can produce images in candlelight, but work better in daylight.

Mixed light Environment where outdoor and indoor light are mixed, causing problems for the white balance system. The solution is to boost one of the light sources at the expense of the other.

Montage Video technique of showing a subject or location by cutting between close-ups of various elements in the scene. The shot order is generally unimportant.

Narrative The art of editing shots together so they progress a story. Good narrative can create interest, humour and suspense.

Neutral shot Shot taken from the most obvious angle, with no intended dramatic effect.

Noise reduction circuitry Circuitry within a piece of hardware, particularly a video processor, that helps eliminate picture interference.

Pulling focus Refocusing from a distant subject in a scene to a close subject in the same shot. Refocusing on a more distant subject is known as throwing focus.

RCTC (rewritable consumer time code) Time code system used on 8mm camcorders. Can be added to a pre-recorded tape.

Setting light Light used to illuminate scenery or background, without lighting the subject.

Soundtrack Area of the tape where the sound is recorded. One track is required for mono recording, two for stereo (left and right).

Strobing Effect caused by high-speed shutter missing out portions of action, resulting in moving subjects appearing to move jerkily.

Sweetening Mixing in additional sound, such as music or sound effects, at the time of editing.

Synchro editing Ensuring more accurate edit points by using a synchro edit lead. This delays the source machine to compensate for the record machine's backspace time.

Sync sound Sound recorded on the camcorder tape at the same time as the picture. All sound relating to actions, such as speech, should be recorded as sync sound. Music and wildtrack can be added later.

Time code System of giving every frame on a video tape an individual label, based on hours, minutes, seconds and frames into the tape. Used to ensure accuracy at the editing stage.

Transitions Various methods of moving from one shot to another. Most basic is the cut, when one shot ends and the next starts in the following frame at full intensity. Others include fades, dissolves, wipes and ripple effects.

Tromboning Overuse of the zoom due to poor technique.

Tungsten light Most indoor lamps use tungsten bulbs with a colour temperature of 3200°K, which have a yellow cast. Video lamps have a slightly higher colour temperature of 3400°K.

Vision mixer Stand alone unit incorporating a genlock, enabling it to mix two video signals.

VITC (vertical integrated time code) Time code system used by VHS camcorders. Can only be recorded during shooting or copying – not added to pre-recorded tape.

White balance Facility of the camcorder to boost colours in the recorded image to compensate for colour casts due to the type of lighting dominant in the scene. Aim is to render white as pure white, regardless of colour cast.

Wildtrack Continuous background sound normally recorded with an audio recorder. When added to the assemble edited video, it adds atmosphere and may help to disguise jump cuts.

Index

A

B

C

D

E